AF378270

The Illustrated History of
LIVERPOOL'S SUBURBS

The Illustrated History of
LIVERPOOL'S SUBURBS

DAVID LEWIS

The City of Liverpool

breedon **books**
PUBLISHING

First published in Great Britain in 2003 by
The Breedon Books Publishing Company Limited
Breedon House, 3 The Parker Centre,
Derby, DE21 4SZ.
Updated 2008

ISBN 978-1-85983-617-0

Printed and bound by Cromwell Press, Trowbridge, Wiltshire.

Contents

ACKNOWLEDGEMENTS

I would like to thank the following people for their help in writing this book. Justine Cook and my parents Reginald and Dorothy Lewis, for their love, enthusiasm and support; the staff at Liverpool Record Office for their time and knowledge; Rupert Harding and Susan Last at Breedon Books for their confidence and commitment; Jeff Young and Sean Halligan for tales of suburban exploration and maps on beer mats; Maria Barrett for past support and present curiosity, and my colleagues at the Directory of Social Change for their interest and stories.

Liverpool Record Office

The City of Liverpool

Liverpool Record Office collects, preserves and makes available archives and local studies material relating to all aspects of the history of the city and its inhabitants.

You can find out about your family history, the history of your house, street and district, famous Liverpool people and landmarks, and much more.

Extensive collections are held dating from the 13th century to the present, some of which are of national and even international significance. They include archives of the City Council and its predecessors, churches, cemeteries, schools, workhouses, families, businesses, trade unions, charities and societies.

Liverpool Record Office is run in conjunction with the Local Studies Library and Merseyside Record Office. This means that there are many collections all available in one place. There is also a major reference and lending library in the same building. The Local Studies Library has thousands of books, street and trade directories from 1766 to 1970, electoral or voters' registers from 1832–1914, 1918–1939 and 1945 onwards, and copies of many local newspapers from 1756 to the present day. There is a large number of street maps and Ordnance Survey maps.

There are significant collections of photographs from the late 19th century onwards. Some of these have been digitised. There is also a fine collection of over 5,000 watercolours.

There are copies of the census returns for Liverpool and the surrounding area and the Wirral from 1841 to 1901, national probate indexes from 1858 to 1951, and copies of the births, marriages and deaths indexes for England and Wales from 1837 to 2000.

We have a range of publications. These include leaflets and lists on many key sources for family and local history. There are also local history books, reproduction maps, and a CD-ROM containing 650 archive photographs and film footage.

We are leading a project for a major digitised history of the Port of Liverpool, its people and the surrounding area at http://www.mersey-gateway.org. This will include 20,000 images.

We welcome the offer of material for safekeeping by deposit or donation.

Liverpool Record Office, Central Library, William Brown Street, Liverpool L3 8EW
Tel: 0151 233 5817/5811
Fax: (for Central Library) 0151 233 5886
Email: RecOffice.central.library@liverpool.gov.uk
Website: www.liverpool.gov.uk

Appointments are essential for consulting some sources – please check before visiting.

The 1768 map of Liverpool by William Yates and George Perry. It is unusual because it shows the surrounding villages as well as the town itself.

Mock beggar
Q
Q
Little Wool ton
Mackits Lane
P
Road to Prescot
Hollands
Farm
Cockshot
orGate
here
Pilch Lane
Gossty
Childwall House
M
Cop
S
Chapel
Wool ton
Sandy lane
R
Boon Field
New lane
Camp
Ash
Summer Hill
Bath
Summer house
Knotty
Thomas Lane
Broad green
Score Lane
Hill House
Allerton Hall
Petticoat Lane
Childwall Heath
Hunts Folly
N
Dowes
Wavertree nook
Childwall Hall
May Place
L
Old Swans
Dodlow hall
Hillpit house
Allerton
Edge Lane
Dry Soil
Lawtons
Wavertree Lane
Wavertree
Rose Lane
Cob Hall
Outacre Lane
O
Fairfield
Bridge House
Raven Bank
Mosley Hill
Aighburgh Hall
Wavertree Hall
Pump House
Old Hall
Green Field
Smithdown Lane
Re servoir
Lodge Lane
Lower Lodge
Otters Pool
Moss Lake
Lodge
New house
Jericho
Observatory
K
Park Lane
Dr Kenions
Park Lane
Park Chapel
Knotts Hole
Runners
Pars
R   I   V   E   R   M   E   R   S   E   Y
Bromborough Pool
Woodside Ferry
Birkhead Abby
Barn
Brickiln-house
Explanation.
A.B. &c.   Parishes and Lordships
Windmills
Stations
Churches
Villages
Seats and Farm Houses
Watermills
Boundaries
Milestones
Rock-house Ferry
Birkhead Pool
O   F   C   H   E   S   H   I   R   E

INTRODUCTION

Liverpool is a very old city. In 2007 it will celebrate the 800th anniversary of the modern founding of the borough and markets by King John, who wanted a port for the trade and conquest of Ireland. But the villages surrounding King John's new town have a far longer history. Some were mentioned in the great Domesday survey of 1086, although famously Liverpool itself was not; at the time it was either not in existence or too small to mention. But many of these villages are far older than Domesday, and their Anglo-Saxon or Norse names suggest a history of use or habitation of over 1,400 years. For centuries of their existence, these were small farming communities, linked to each other by farm tracks and lanes. Many of these lanes became metalled roads, and are still in existence. The villages grew as the roads and communications improved with the little port of Liverpool, but the increased communication also produced new settlements, with districts growing around coaching inns on important road junctions.

The colossal expansion of the city under the Victorians swallowed these outlying villages and turned them into suburbs. In some cases the heart of the settlement remained, but in most instances the village was dissolved by the city and only the roads (which gave the district its importance) were kept. The Victorian city spread across geographical barriers previously thought insurmountable, such as the Mosslake and the Great Heath, and the farmland between the old villages was built over. There are still remnants of the old rural landscape in places such as West Derby or Wavertree, but in most cases these villages have very few buildings from before the Victorian era. In time many of the crowded streets of the old city were cleared because they were insanitary, and many people were moved out to bright new suburban estates beyond the Victorian fringe. The 20th century saw Liverpool develop new industries far from the river, and build huge car plants and factories on the flat lands to the east and south-east of the city. These too needed workers, and large suburban townships were built a long way from the city centre, in many cases building around or over an existing village.

The nature of its expansion has meant that, like London, Liverpool is a city of urban villages, a point well made by Derek Whale in his trilogy, *Lost Villages of Liverpool.* I was saddened to hear of Mr Whale's death during the preparation of this book in the summer of 2003. His books are well-written and informative and helped me discover the overlooked history of Liverpool's outlying districts.

I have taken 'suburbs' to mean largely residential districts around the city centre and with very little 'infrastructure' of their own, although this proved to be a shifting definition. The choice was, to an extent, a personal one, since not all suburbs could be covered; my brief was to cover the older districts and not the history of post-1945 expansion, so the huge 'new towns' of Kirkby and Runcorn and the dormitory towns of Maghull, Prescot, Crosby and Formby are not covered in the book, nor are 'second growth' suburbs such as Huyton or Page Moss, despite their interesting histories. I have concentrated on the older 'inner city' suburbs, what might be called 'first growth' districts, from Speke and Garston in the south to Bootle and Walton in the north, and as far east as West Derby and Fazakerley.

Further Reading

Many of the suburbs have writers who wrote extensively on local landscape and history. Articulate and informed, they provide a fascinating sidelight on the city's growth. Some wrote at a time when the tide of 'suburbanisation' was just beginning and was resented for its haste and cost – if they were only just in time to record the demolition of a mediaeval farm building or small manor house, for example. Other local topographers went to the level of analysing field names to find lost folk-records of Dark Age skirmishes between 'Briton' and 'Dane', on fields now buried beneath 1930s mock-Tudor houses and neat gardens. It is a pity that many of these books or small pamphlets are now out of print, but many are available in the Records Office in Liverpool Central Library. Derek Whale's trilogy *Lost Villages of Liverpool* has already been mentioned. I found this a useful guide and source of stories and personalities; it should be available with maps and printed on waterproof paper for the use of urban explorers. I also found other more general city histories and architectural guides useful, and a reading list has been added to the end of each chapter.

AIGBURTH AND GARSTON

Aigburth

Aigburth covers a large part of south Liverpool, between the Dingle and Garston, and meets Allerton beneath the tall trees of Mossley Hill. The place-name is Anglo-Saxon, and translates into modern English as 'place of the oaks'. Aigburth is still a very leafy suburb. It is a curious mixture of housing and parks, busy roads and quiet woodland; it includes the bohemian bedsits of Lark Lane and the old iron village of St Michael's, as well as the woods at Otterspool and the sedate 1930s suburbia of Aigburth Road.

When the Anglo-Saxons were exploring this region 1,500 years ago, 'Aigburth' was an area of heath and woodland covering the gentle slope down to the river. It

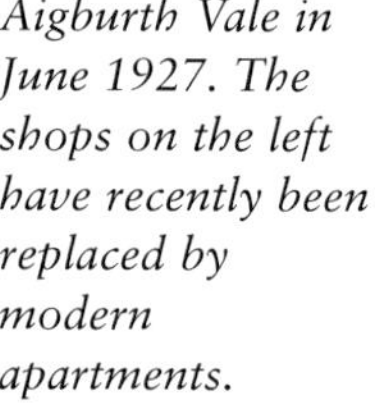

Aigburth Vale in June 1927. The shops on the left have recently been replaced by modern apartments.

Aigburth Vale on 22 June 1927, looking towards Sefton Park. This view is largely unchanged today.

is possible that the village was near a sacred grove in the trees, but whether it was a Germanic settlement or simply renamed by them is unclear. This earliest settlement seems to have been on the high ground of Aigburth Vale alongside the Osklesbrook, the small river that rises in Wavertree and runs through Sefton Park, down the Vale, and into the Mersey. The area of Aigburth Vale furthest from Aigburth Road was known as the village until the 1960s, when a lot of older property was demolished and replaced by the slightly utilitarian apartment blocks that now stand between Sefton Park and Victoria Road, straddling the Vale. A long avenue of chestnut trees is all that survives of this older Aigburth Vale, running from the crossroads with Elmswood Road to Queens Drive. The Victorians discovered Roman coins on the banks of the small river, but other evidence for them here is slight.

From the beginning of the 13th century the Osklesbrook formed one of the boundaries of King John's hunting forest of Toxteth Park. A mediaeval hunting lodge was demolished as recently as the 1860s to make way for Otterspool railway station, now a private residence. When local writer Robert Griffiths explored the park in the early 20th century, pieces of mediaeval masonry from the lodge were still visible near the railway viaduct. Carved masonry still forms part of the low wall alongside the main road through the park, but whether it came from King John's lodge or not is difficult to tell.

Toxteth Park was broken up in the late 16th century, and much of the land was sold off to Puritan families. They transformed the hunting forest into farmland, and left their mark on Toxteth and Aigburth, as many of the roads still follow field boundaries laid down 300 years ago. They consciously chose to reflect their theology in the landscape and, as well as building the Ancient Chapel in the Dingle, they renamed the Osklesbrook the River Jordan, and laid out the farm called Jericho. For many years after the park was broken up the old hunting lodge near Jericho Lane was a farmhouse, and the astronomer Jeremiah Horrocks was born there in 1619. He is commemorated by plaques in both the Ancient Chapel and the church of St Michael in the Hamlet.

The Catholic Church owned huge swathes of south Lancashire until the Reformation, and the monks of Whalley Abbey owned much of Aigburth and Garston. They let much of the farmland to tenants, but also farmed it themselves and built extensive farm buildings here. Most have gone, but Stanlawe Grange on Aigburth Hall Road survives, and is possibly the oldest inhabited building in Liverpool. The monks supposedly rowed across the river (then wider and shallower than today), and there is a modern Monksferry Road near the river commemorating this. They valued the land for its richness and for centuries Aigburth was an agricultural district, a landscape of fields and woods and small farms with sandstone farmhouses.

The Victorians saw great potential in south Liverpool, and began its transformation from farmland to suburb by building three private estates in the 1840s, in what was then open country. Fulwood Park, Grassendale Park and Cressington Park were built off the main Aigburth Road for Liverpool's merchants, and enabled them to be within easy reach of the town but without its inconveniences. The houses are set apart in large gardens and have kept an air of gentle exclusivity, with their wide roads and mature trees; the estates are still quiet and peaceful, and Grassendale and Cressington have a pleasant promenade along the river. James Kennedy, who on the opening day of the Liverpool & Manchester Railway drove the *Rocket* to get help for William Huskisson, lived on Eaton Road and died in 1886, aged 96. The poet William Watson lived on Salisbury Road at the end of the century. He is largely forgotten today, but was considered important enough by Prime Minister Gladstone to be granted £200 from the Civil List on the death of Tennyson.

The biggest green space in Aigburth is Sefton Park, which was laid out in 1872. The beautiful Palm House has been restored, and the park has miles of elegant

sweeping walks though woodland and open fields. It is Liverpool's greatest park and has always been a playground for the city's children, as well as being popular for big parades and events; before World War One it was used for military reviews. The plots around the park were sold in the 1870s to offset the building costs, so Sefton Park is surrounded by large Victorian houses, now mainly converted into flats. With its fanciful 'Gothick' lodges, fairies' dell under the ornate iron bridge, and great lake and woods, Sefton is a very attractive park. Until recently Peter Pan was here, a bronze copy of the George Frampton statue in London's Kensington Gardens, complete with adoring Wendy and a host of tiny bronze animals. But the Victorian builders went even further, and surrounded Peter with some of the magic of Never-Never Land. There used to be tiny cannons from one of the royal yachts, a thatched Wendy House with a top hat perched jauntily on top and an old Cunard lifeboat transformed into Captain Hook's ship. At the time of writing Peter's statue is in Liverpool's award-winning Conservation Centre for a clean-up and to restore

Aigburth Vale tram waiting room in the summer of 1908. These Edwardian passengers seem very conscious of being photographed.

Sefton Park lake on a snowy day in December 1912. A reminder of how the park looked before the 1960s tower blocks ruined the horizon.

John Brodie, City Engineer, and his chauffeur in 1907. This splendid photograph was taken at Brodie's house on Ullet Road, which is now marked with a blue plaque.

one or two missing animals. But there is still an aviary here, and a café, and until recently the crossroads opposite was guarded by a statue of Eros over a vast bronze fountain, a copy of the more famous Eros in Piccadilly. He too had to be taken to the Conservation Centre as the bronze glue holding him to the fountain was crumbling. They named the centre's café after him, and local hopes are still high that he will one day return to the fountain.

The Victorians also built large estates in Aigburth; some are still in private hands but most have gone completely, leaving only echoes. The modern Carnatic Halls on Mossley Hill remember an older house built with the proceeds of privateering in the Napoleonic Wars; Sudley (the most complete of these estates) was for years the home of a ship-owning family, the Holts, and their art collection and house are now open to the public. And Otterspool Park,

down on the waterfront, still has the ornate plants and shrubs of the landscaped park, but the great house has gone; it stood where the old café now is, with only a low balustrade and crumbling stonework to show where it once stood. Staying with the wealthy family who owned the estate, George Stephenson once built a model railway line through the park, and as if remembering past glories Otterspool has a brooding atmosphere even on the brightest days; the woods are thick and strangely quiet, and the mood is wary rather than peaceful.

The red-brick terraced housing, which makes up much of the modern district, is probably the Victorians' greatest legacy in Aigburth. The streets stretch from the Dingle to the cricket ground at Riversdale Road, and are the backbone of the area's housing stock. (Two of Liverpool's famous comedians grew up in these Victorian houses. Tommy Handley was born on Riversdale Road on the border with Garston, and in later life Arthur Askey remembered cycling from Aigburth to school at the Liverpool Institute, past the building site that was slowly becoming the Anglican

Aigburth Boulevard in 1908, when horse traffic outnumbered motor cars.

A quiet day on Aigburth Road in 1947. The tramlines have gone but the view is largely unchanged today.

Jericho Lane in June 1929. The building on the left is Jericho Farm. This road still runs through playing fields today.

Early catering facilities at Otterspool Promenade in May 1951.

Cathedral.) In recent years these old houses have become desirable again, and Aigburth Vale in particular is a popular place to live, with new businesses and bars opening to replace traditional shops. The site of the old Aigburth Vale Girls' High School has become expensive luxury flats, with footballers and even the manager of Liverpool Football Club enjoying the view into Sefton Park as their wealthy Victorian predecessors did.

Lark Lane and St Michael's Hamlet

Lark Lane is a self-contained modern urban village, connecting Aigburth Road with Sefton Park, and is surrounded by tree-lined streets of large Victorian houses. Many of these houses are now flats, occupied by artists and students attracted by the Lane's shops and bars, and the gentle air of faded bohemia. The roads around Lark Lane were laid out from the 1840s onwards and seem to extend the leafy promise of Sefton Park, but the later housing built on the opposite side of Aigburth Road is very different and consists of long straight streets of terraced houses. Yet embedded in these is St Michael's Hamlet, an early 19th-century village purpose-built by a local iron founder, John Cragg. Cragg worked with the eccentric architect Thomas Rickman to build Liverpool's cast-iron churches, and developed Rickman's ideas to prefabricate houses. He laid out the hamlet around the cast-iron church of St Michael's, and created a district of Gothic Revival houses with everything possible made out of iron; windows, doorframes, fireplaces, the skeleton of the church itself. Even the waterfront here is known as 'the cast-iron shore' and was immortalised by the Beatles in their song *Glass Onion*. St Michael's Hamlet has retained its urban village atmosphere, with quiet streets and chestnut trees in the gardens of large attractive houses, and has been a conservation area since 1968.

Otterspool House. Only the steps and balustrade remain today.

Otterspool

The 'otter's pool' was the mouth of the old Osklesbrook, which widened as it flowed into the Mersey. It was once famous for salmon, which perhaps attracted otters, but today Otterspool is famous for the Promenade. This is a landscape of open grassland and secluded benches, running alongside the broad Mersey with splendid views to the mountains of Wales and the heavy industry of Ellesmere Port. It was originally suggested by the far-sighted City Engineer John Brodie (who lived at Aigburth Hall) in 1919, and was laid out in the 1940s and 1950s when the spoil from the first Mersey road tunnel, and the city's refuse, were put to good use in strengthening the riverbanks. There is still a small recycling depot there today.

The Promenade now stretches from the separate waterfront of Grassendale to the Albert Dock, but the most famous stretch is at Otterspool, where a finely chiselled slate plaque marks its official opening in 1950. From the start it has been a popular

Otterspool Promenade in July 1951, shortly after it had opened.

'lung' for south Liverpool, good for flying kites, walking, picnics and as a safe place for children to play. The Promenade is well landscaped, with short paths connecting the riverside walk with the roads above, and although some of the architecture and landscaping is looking its age, the 'Prom' is well used and still very popular.

The idea of reusing the city's waste reached its height when the old landfill site was dramatically transformed in the aftermath of the disturbances in Toxteth in 1981. Otterspool was chosen as the site for the first International Garden Festival, which was to be the first of a series of festivals that would use horticulture to kick-start investment and tourism in deprived inner cities. Many countries donated gardens and sculpture and the landscape was transformed from urban blight to parkland and woods, centred on a riverside walkway and a huge concert arena. New roads were built, as were large car parks and even a riverside public house. The Festival ran in the summer of 1984, and was a great success, with large numbers of people visiting the gardens from all over the world, and seeing Liverpool as a tourist destination for the first time.

In the years since 1984 the site has become something of a white elephant. Houses were built on part of the site, and the arena was used for a time as an indoor play and leisure centre. But most of the generously donated gardens and planting have run wild, and the sculpture stands sadly in thick woodland. The landmark arena is abandoned and in poor condition, and only the public house and the promenade alongside the river are as the designers planned. Arguably the International Garden Festival began the massive regeneration of the south Liverpool waterfront area, but the site itself is abandoned and overgrown and the debate to decide its future goes on.

Garston

The Anglo-Saxons gave this area the name 'Gaerstun', which means 'grass or grazing settlement', and presumably used it for raising livestock. There is little evidence for earlier settlement apart from the so-called 'Roman pavement', which was discovered during excavations for sewers in 1855. It was situated approximately 300 yards east of St Mary's church, an area now covered by 1930s housing. The pavement lay seven feet below the surface and was running in a south-easterly direction, towards Garston or Hale. It was formed of large and small

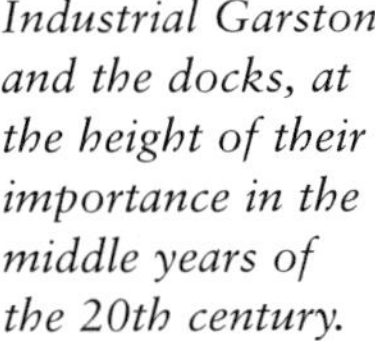

Industrial Garston and the docks, at the height of their importance in the middle years of the 20th century.

boulders laid perfectly flat, without any camber, and many of the stones were worn smooth by traffic.

For 300 years until the Reformation, the monks of Whalley and Stanlawe Abbeys owned Garston. They grew cereal crops here, and built granaries and water mills to process them. For most of its recorded history Garston was a patchwork of fields and woodland, and as recently as the 1840s there were only a handful of roads across the fields, most of which are still there; Garston Old Road, Church Road, St Mary's Road. It was the meeting of these two roads that formed the village centre, with a straggle of houses along these lanes and the small ponds that led down to the river. For many years Garston had extensive fisheries and watermills, which were fed by a stream that had its source in the higher ground of Allerton. Derek Whale comments that this watercourse was channelled into an underground culvert as the town grew over it, and was seen for the first time in decades when it was exposed during work for the Garston bypass in the autumn of 1982.

Garston has lost most of its very old buildings. It had Garston Old Hall, for

Speke Road, looking towards the match factory, on a quiet day in May 1928. The factory has recently been renovated as apartments as part of the regeneration of the area.

example, which dated from the 15th century and stood on the site of an even earlier manor house. The Old Hall stood on the 'Monk's Field' on Garston Old Road, and was demolished early in the 19th century. The oldest buildings in modern Garston are churches, with the old Methodist chapel now in the schoolyard of St Francis of Assisi clearly marked on maps from the 1840s. A church dedicated to St Winifred or

Groes Road in July 1907. The newly built houses have farmland at the end of the street.

Wilfrid stood on the site of St Michael's church from at least 1225, and for centuries was known as the Ancient Chapel of Garston. (Only Toxteth now has an 'Ancient Chapel', but once Garston and Wavertree possessed 'ancient' churches.) The village sat along the crossroads, and there were mills and fishing sites, but apart from this handful of buildings all Garston was fields and woodland until the 19th century.

Tram track laying on Sinclair Street in October 1914.

In the decades following the Great Famine of the late 1840s the Irish arrived in Liverpool in their tens of thousands, and many settled in Woolton and Garston to work in the quarries and the burgeoning dock system. The 1870s saw a further explosion of building in the little village, with streets of neat red-brick houses and larger villas being built. Many are still in existence today, with the streets around Wellington Road and Clarendon Road, and the neat terraces running off Bowden Road, still being desirable places to live.

Modern Garston was established by the arrival of the railway and the docks. The earliest docks were built in the mid-18th century, to repair small coastal vessels that carried Cheshire salt and coal from St Helens down the Mersey and around the coast. These small concerns were overshadowed and then obliterated by the massive dock and railway system created from the 1850s onwards. At its height the Garston dock system employed 1,000 people and had 93 miles of railway linking the docks, which brought international cargoes into the country. Working conditions were harsh, and the London and North Western Railway had the first mortuary in

Garston, so common were deaths on the docks. The docks are safer today, but mechanisation has meant that the system is not the great employer it once was. Jack Jones, the former general secretary of the Transport and General Workers' Union, was once a docker in Garston, as was his father. The family lived in a two-up two-down house on York Street, which Jack Jones described as 'a long street of poor and mean terraced houses' near to the 'muddy playground' of the river.

The township of Garston was incorporated into Liverpool in November 1902. Aigburth and Allerton expanded during the mid-20th century, building long roads of semi-detached housing, and the borders with neighbouring suburbs were blurred. Today Garston is no longer as separate as it once was. The hub of the district is still the crossroads of St Mary's Road and Church Road, as it has been for centuries, although the bypass erected in the early 1980s both deadened and revitalised the old village heart; deadened because the lack of passing trade has amputated Old St Mary's Road and killed many small businesses, but revitalised because a quieter village centre has meant more pedestrianisation. The village centre has recently been refurbished, and although much of Garston is run-down and neglected, in recent years some areas have become popular places to live, and for good reason. Garston has a stable population, interesting and attractive buildings, and a large park and sports centre. It is well placed for access both to Liverpool city centre and the national motorway network. The partial pedestrianisation of the village centre has created a pleasant centre in which to work and play, and it is to be hoped that Garston can attract sufficient investment and interest to become a real urban village, while retaining its own identity within the larger pattern of Liverpool's suburbs.

Further reading

Joseph Boult, *The Historical Topography of Aigburth and Garston*, Lancashire and Cheshire Historical Society Transactions, 1868.

Robert Griffiths, *The History of the Royal and Ancient Park of Toxteth*, reprinted 2000.

R. Millington, *The House in the Park*, Liverpool, 1957

Derek Whale, *Lost Villages of Liverpool*, Part I, 1985.

ALLERTON

Allerton is a wealthy suburb, some four or five miles out from the city centre. It is dissected by Queens Drive and by other large avenues connecting it with Garston, Aigburth, and the city centre. It is a stable and quite conservative district, and with its broad avenues of mock-Tudor housing and large mature gardens seems the epitome of the bland city suburb. But Joseph of Arimathea, Paul McCartney, Robin Hood and Edward Burne-Jones have links with Allerton, some mythical, some less so. One of Liverpool's famous novelists once lived here, and the district has a surprising number of standing stones, as well as memories of the great Liverpool merchants of the 19th century – and Liverpool's oldest tree.

A performance at the open air theatre, Calderstones Park, in August 1958.

The oldest man-made structure in Liverpool was a prehistoric burial mound, which stood where Menlove Avenue is today. For many years the mound was the official boundary between Wavertree and Allerton. The mound was excavated in the late 18th century and the contents – supposedly some urn burials – were stored in a barn, where over the years they were broken and the contents dispersed. This shameful treatment of the city's oldest structure resulted in the Calderstones, huge pieces of sooty sandstone decorated with spirals and cup markings, once the walls and roof of the burial mound.

The stones have given their name to Calderstones Park, a large and attractive park that was formed from the private estates of two of Liverpool's Victorian merchant families. John Bibby once lived in the Harthill estate, although nothing now remains of his great house, and the Mansion House in the park, now council offices, was once the home of the Brocklebank family. Calderstones Park has the Allerton Oak, an ancient tree supposedly 1,000 years old, which would place it neatly at the end of the first millennium. The Hundred Court was presumed to sit in session under this tree, although it would of course have been a sapling when they did so!

The Calderstones themselves have been moved a number of times from their original location, and are now housed in one of the surviving glasshouses of the Botanic Gardens. The gardens were moved to Allerton from Edge Lane in the mid-20th century and were shamefully closed by the council in the 1980s. It is a further shame that the Calderstones are rarely open to the public, and do not form the

Smithdown Place. 'The shelter in the middle of the roundabout' is obscured by buses on 14 May 1957. This view is largely unchanged today.

centrepiece of a visitor centre, perhaps with the urns from the prehistoric Wavertree cemetery, and the city's oldest structures more appropriately celebrated.

Allerton has quite a scattering of monoliths. A hundred feet or so from the Calderstones stands the short pillar known as 'Jesse Hartley's Stone'. The stone was supposedly a sample sent to Hartley when he was considering materials for the Liverpool docks, and it stands today in the centre of a path connecting the Calderstones with the flowerbeds surrounding the glasshouses. This modern standing stone has been well placed, and has all the eerie beauty of an ancient monolith. And Allerton has another 'ancient' standing stone carved from the local sandstone. The deep grooves on 'Robin Hood's Stone' were supposedly carved by Robin sharpening his arrows, although it is more likely that local archers carved them, perhaps during target practice in the reign of Henry VIII. Peter Howell Williams quotes the intriguing possibility that retainers of Sir Richard Molyneux may have practised archery here before embarking for the battle of Agincourt in 1415, but adds that this is 'mere conjecture'. Today the stone stands quietly behind sturdy railings on Booker Avenue, together with a plaque recording its history in some detail.

Booker Avenue under construction, on a hot day in July 1933.

It is appropriate that Hartley's stone is near the Harthill estate, since Jesse Hartley's daughter Fanny married John Bibby. He commemorated her life in true Victorian fashion by building a church, the splendid All Hallows', which stands on Allerton Road just beyond the old Harthill estate. All Hallows' is a very beautiful church on a quiet stretch of Allerton Road. It is built of sandstone, which gives it a rugged, solid appearance, and its fine 'Somerset' tower is a local landmark. The church opened in 1876 and is justly famous for its collection of windows by Edward Burne-Jones. In the small churchyard outside is a sapling from the Glastonbury Thorn, supposedly brought to England as the staff of Joseph of Arimathea.

There is a small 17th-century farmhouse still surviving off Mather Avenue, but most of the oldest buildings in Allerton are the large houses built by Liverpool's merchants in the 19th century. The newly rich took the ideas of the landed gentry, and a large number of stately homes were laid out in a great swathe of south Liverpool, from Aigburth and Allerton to Woolton. They were designed by the

Springwood Avenue under construction in September 1921.

Dovedale Road and the tower of the Baptist church in July 1921.

leading local architects of the day: Thomas Harrison, Harvey Lonsdale Elmes, Alfred Waterhouse. Even George Gilbert Scott and Richard Norman Shaw built for Liverpool's rich at this time. Much of this legacy has gone, been 'wantonly thrown away' in Quentin Hughes's words. The Mansion House in Calderstones Park remains, as does Waterhouse's vast Allerton Priory, which is now being restored and adapted into apartments for Liverpool's new rich, but most have been built over or simply demolished. They have left us acres of parkland and sad ruins like Harrison's Allerton Park, dating from 1815 and a burnt-out shell now surrounded by Allerton Golf Course. On the lawn in front of its overgrown portico stands a great sandstone obelisk, which gave it the alternative name of Obelisk House. The column, however, is far older than Allerton Park, and was erected to mark the termination of a great avenue of beeches planted as a vista from Allerton Hall, across Woolton Road. The Hall has a longer history than the neighbouring Victorian estates and is possibly mediaeval in origin. William Roscoe once owned this fine house, until bankruptcy forced him to sell it. Today it is a restaurant and pub, and the only one of these grand estates to be fully enjoyed by the general public.

Mather Avenue and All Souls' church in October 1935.

Victorian maps show Allerton as a patchwork of farmland and large estates, a landscape essentially unchanged for centuries. Even at the beginning of the 20th century the area was largely open fields, with farms on Allerton Road and the Liverpool Polo Ground on 'Taggart Avenue'. As with most of Liverpool, the 20th century saw Allerton transformed from a rural district to a city suburb, with the fields built up with mile upon mile of semi-detached houses. Yet the earlier landscape is still very much in evidence, as much of Allerton is still open parkland or playing fields; the 1930s houses have large gardens, and mature trees line the great boulevards connecting the district with the city and Garston. Even in the 1950s when Richard Whittington-Egan wrote about the district there were still farmers working in Allerton, and one of them remembered the writer Nicholas Monsarrat, the author of *The Cruel Sea*, living off Greenhill Road.

The most famous modern inhabitant of Allerton is Paul McCartney, whose family lived on Forthlin Road. The house has recently been acquired by the National Trust, who have stripped away the modern paintwork and restored the house to how it could have looked when

The tangled boughs of the Allerton Oak, Liverpool's oldest tree.

the McCartneys lived there in the 1950s. The area has changed little since then, and the walk between this house and John Lennon's old home on Menlove Avenue would be familiar to Lennon and McCartney today. Indeed much of modern Allerton would be familiar to them, and the area is still saturated with obscure Beatles history, from schools and family homes to early performance venues such as the Dovedale Towers pub. Penny Lane too is in Allerton, and attracts thousands of fans every year to see the 'shelter in the middle of the roundabout', the bank and the barber's shop. Lennon's mother's family, the Stanleys, lived in Newcastle Road, a street still visited by well-informed Beatles fans today. His school, Quarrybank High School, still stands next to Calderstones Park and gave its name to Lennon's first band, the Quarrymen.

The heart of modern Allerton is the shopping district of Allerton Road, basically a stretch of shops, restaurants and bars on the arterial route from Garston to the city centre. This central road is busy and congested with traffic but, thanks to the city authority's acquisition of the remains of the big estates, it is still possible to

Jesse Hartley's Stone, Calderstones Park.

walk from the busy shops of Allerton Road all the way into Woolton and over towards Hunts Cross without crossing a new road, although these old lanes are far busier with cars than they have ever been.

Further reading
Quentin Hughes, *Liverpool City of Architecture,* Liverpool, 1999
Richard Whittington-Egan, *Liverpool Soundings,* Liverpool, 1969
Peter Howell Williams, *Liverpolitana,* Liverpool, 1971

ANFIELD

Anfield lies between Tuebrook and Walton, Everton and Clubmoor, and because it is the home of Liverpool Football Club is a name familiar to millions across the world. But it is a fine Victorian suburb with a rich heritage of interesting buildings, as well as the great open spaces of Stanley Park and the necropolis of Anfield Cemetery.

'Anfield' is a corruption of 'hangfield' or 'the hanging fields', a reference to the long sloping farmland behind the little village of Everton, and for many centuries this was an agricultural district. Anfield is still the district behind Everton's high ridge, sloping down towards Tuebrook and West Derby, and many of its principal roads have remained unchanged for at least 200 years, and probably far longer.

An empty Utting Avenue in 1924, before the full development of the Clubmoor estate.

William Yates and George Perry, surveying the environs of 'Leverpool' in 1768, recorded 'Ann Field', Townsend Lane and Rocky Lane, as well as the unnamed Priory Road running to the vanished hamlet of Mare Green on the site of Stanley Park. These roads cross farmland but at the very top of the hill the soil was poor and largely heath and gorse; this is reflected in the local word 'breck', meaning heath land, which has given its name to many roads across the district.

Anfield was largely built up in the late 19th century to provide working-class housing for the city, and the miles of neat red-brick terracing are still largely intact; only on the borders with Everton are there more modern housing areas. Here larger Victorian properties were mistakenly demolished in the 1960s, and the area has yet to recover.

The heart of Anfield today is the busy arterial route and shopping district of Breck Road. Here the slope of the old hangfield becomes apparent, and on a clear day the Pennines can be seen. The Victorian buildings are tall, with shops on the ground floor and flats above. They are built of the attractive hard red-brick and

Traffic and roadworks outside Anfield Cemetery in September 1937.

Breck Road shops on a sombre day in December 1935.

The neat entrance to Anfield Crematorium in 1908, the year it was taken over from a private company by Liverpool Corporation.

terracotta detailing that can be found throughout the city, but heavy traffic and the

terracotta detailing that can be found throughout the city, but heavy traffic and the
bustle of shoppers on the narrow pavements makes appreciation difficult. Yet the
best of Anfield's Victorian heritage is here, with the Gothic fantasy of the Richmond
pub, the landmark church of the Holy Trinity with its fine octagonal spire and rich
carving, and the austere façade of Richmond Baptist church, designed in 1865 by
James Picton.

But possibly the biggest Victorian achievement in Anfield was Liverpool Football
Club. It is well known that Everton and Liverpool grew out of the same football
team attached to St Domingo Methodist Church in 1878. The teams played on
Stanley Park, then recently laid out, and only split into two distinct clubs in the
early 1890s. Both clubs have had major national and international successes, and
attract good-natured fanaticism. It is a sign of the dignity and tolerance of the clubs'
fans that they have never needed to be separated at matches; perhaps the greatest
sign of this was at the memorable 1986 FA cup final between the two city teams,
when reds and blues mixed happily on Wembley's terraces and the chant of
'Merseyside, Merseyside' rolled around the ground. Liverpool's old stadium

*The chapel and
new columbarium
at Anfield
Cemetery on a
sunny day in
August 1954.*

St Domingo Pit, Breckfield Road,
1937. The lamppost remains, and
the cinema is now a social club,
but the houses were demolished
and replaced in the 1960s.

Stanley Park palm house and bandstand in 1906.

between Walton Breck Road and Anfield Road is now too small for the needs of a modern football team, and there is talk of the club moving to a purpose-built site on Stanley Park, which famously separates Liverpool's ground from Everton's ground, Goodison Park.

Stanley Park was laid out in the late 1860s and was dreamed up by Edward Robson, the Corporation Architect. He designed the massive Gothic garden pavilions, but the local architect/builders firm of T.D. Barry built the park. The Corporation bought a number of small estates on what were then the fringes of Liverpool, and Walton Lodge, the Woodlands estate and 'a small row of houses fronting Priory Lane' were cleared for the new park. The public saw the benefits immediately, and in addition to the boating lake and aviaries, the park was celebrated for its views of the 'Cumberland, Westmoreland and Yorkshire hills' especially when 'the state of the atmosphere and the time of the day are favourable'. The park opened in 1870 and on a clear day the Pennines are still clearly visible today, although much of Stanley Park is now dedicated to football. It is a shame that the imposing glasshouse is presently derelict, after a brief resurgence as a restaurant.

On the other side of Priory Road stands Anfield Cemetery, once described as 'the Père Lachaise of Liverpool'. The cemetery was designed by architects Lucy & Littler working with Edward Kemp, and opened in 1863. Anfield Cemetery is a great Victorian necropolis, with imposing avenues, stately drives, and even a set of catacombs. William Herdman, the great Liverpool artist, is buried here, and so is the London artist Jacob Stone. Sportsmen are well represented, especially boxers, including Jem Mace who died in 1910 and was described as the 'father of British boxing, and the first and greatest glove fighter of them all.' Ike Bradley, the bantamweight, was buried not far away in 1951. Past stars of Liverpool and Everton football clubs are here in abundance, near enough to hear the roars from across Stanley Park on a Saturday afternoon; Robert Kenworthy, Fred Parry, George Fleming. There are military dead too, veterans of old imperial conflicts: the Indian Mutiny, the Crimea, the Zulu Wars, even

Rich carving on the gateposts of Holy Trinity church, Breck Road.

Waterloo. Colonel Ellison lies here, the architect of the Adelphi Hotel. So does T.J. Hughes, whose London Road store is still going strong. Canon Thomas Major Lester is buried in Anfield, one half of the first Catholic-Anglican partnership in the city; with Father Nugent he worked tirelessly to help poor and destitute children. Perhaps most moving is the memorial to the dead of the Blitz. Nearly 4,000 civilians were killed in Liverpool during World War Two, and over 500 are buried in Anfield: nearly 400 were unidentified.

With the building of Queens Drive in the middle years of the 20th century, Anfield stretched across the more level ground to the east, and the old Victorian city rubbed up against the new inter-war optimism of Clubmoor and Norris Green.

Today Anfield is a run-down district, and is not a fashionable or glamorous place to live or work. Unlike Everton, however, it has retained much of its Victorian housing stock. Two and three-storey red-brick townhouses with terracotta details are the norm here, and the needless demolition of the 1960s has left little impact on the area. It is hoped that if Liverpool Football Club move to a new location on Stanley Park, then the move will trigger a large amount of rejuvenation for the area. It is to be hoped that many of these elegant houses are retained and renovated and that the character of this attractive Victorian area is not thoughtlessly destroyed.

Further reading

Derek Whale, *Lost Villages of Liverpool*, Part II, 1985

'Zoilus', *Wanderings in Anfield*, Porcupine, Vol. 20, 1878. A strangely jaundiced view of the new suburb.

BOOTLE

Bootle forms the dockside link in the chain of modern suburbs that rings Liverpool today, but it has a proud and distinct history independent of the city. Old civic pride runs deep, and most Bootle people would not claim that their district was merely a suburb of Liverpool. Yet the city's pull is a strong one, and today many Bootle residents travel into Liverpool to work.

It is possible that the earliest people living here were Anglians from Northumbria, who settled here in AD 613 after the battle of Chester, but hard evidence for this is scarce. The small township was in existence by the time of the Domesday survey in 1086, when it was called Boltelai, from the Anglo-Saxon 'botl' meaning a building or settlement of some importance.

Bootle was a small fishing village and later a seaside resort, with miles of golden sands, and for many years the town also supplied Liverpool with fresh water. At the beginning of the 18th century the area was bought by the Earl of Derby (of the Stanley family) who began to lay out the formal streets, named after the colleges of Oxford and Cambridge, that are still in existence today. The oldest building in modern Bootle is an old hunting lodge belonging to the Stanley family; this stone building stands on Merton Road opposite Christ Church and a rainwater head bearing the family crest of the eagle and child is visible nearby.

As the Liverpool docks crept northwards along the waterfront in the mid-19th century, Bootle grew anxious to preserve its independence and in December 1868 purchased a Charter of Incorporation. This was 'brought in triumph into the new borough in an open coach pulled by four grey horses accompanied by postillions and outriders. At the boundary on Derby Road the carriage was met by a brass band and large crowd which wound its way round the borough until the charter was read out in public,' according to local writer Andrew Richardson.

The transition from seaside village to dockside town is marked by William Forwood, later Mayor of

Traffic duty, Derby Road, December 1957. Presumably the policeman is testing his reflective clothing, as traffic seems in short supply.

Liverpool, who lived in the area as a child. 'I remember the grand trees which encircled Bootle Hall and overarched Marsh Lane,' he wrote in 1910. 'The trees extended down to the seashore where Miller's Castle stood sentinel, a modern building remarkable for its keep and battlemented walls.' Seaforth at the time was 'a very prettily wooded village', and wrecks on the Bootle and Seaforth shores were 'quite common occurrences.' 'The farmers in the district fenced their fields with timber from ships stranded on the shore, and the villagers were not above pilfering their cargoes,' he wrote.

As a very young child, William Forwood watched Brunel's steamship the SS *Great Britain* sail down the Mersey from his home, and he was also fortunate in knowing many of the gentry of the district. These included William Ewart Gladstone, the great Victorian Prime Minister, whose father largely built Seaforth. When, in 1893, Forwood told Gladstone about the new Overhead Railway and its station in Seaforth, Gladstone replied 'I remember as a boy catching what we called "snigs" in the Rimrose Brook… and I played cricket in the adjoining field, from whence in the far, far distance we could see the smoke of Liverpool.' Gladstone also famously remembered seeing wild roses bloom in the middle of what is now Bootle.

The docks brought prosperity to the new borough, and paid for the ornate Town Hall, the Art Gallery, the Police and Law Courts, still a symbol of Sefton civic pride. But in World War Two the docks were targeted by the Luftwaffe, and Bootle suffered the heaviest and most destructive bombing of anywhere in Britain, which caused appalling loss of life and property. 'Such was the extent of the damage,' wrote Andrew Richardson, 'that the 1939 population figure of 80,000 was reduced by 1941 to a daytime figure of 30,000, with only 10,000 remaining in the area at night.' He adds that over 2,000 houses were destroyed, and of the remaining 15,000 only 40 escaped damage altogether.

Since 1945 much of central Bootle has been rebuilt, and there are no longer the bombsite gaps in the landscape, but much of Victorian Bootle was lost in the war. Although a number of Government departments housed branches in the rebuilding, their

Coffee House Bridge, Irlam Road, on a quiet day in June 1903.

The old and the new in modern Bootle.

Bootle civic pride – the Town Hall on a misty day in 2003.

stark 1960s modernism sits a little uneasily with the Victorian survivors, a contrast reflected in much of modern Bootle. The docks now generate electricity through the new wind farm, and process more cargo than ever before, but employ fewer people; there are modern industrial estates alongside terraced streets; and huge glass and steel office blocks tower over delicate churches or sturdy Victorian mansions.

Further Reading
Bootle Community Archives Project, *The Bootle File*, 1995.
William Forwood, *Recollections of a Busy Life*, Liverpool, 1910.
Andrew Richardson, *Central Bootle – A Walking Tour of the Buildings and Monuments,* 1993.

CHILDWALL

Childwall stretches from the Fiveways junction on Queens Drive to Black Woods on the borders with Woolton, and is almost entirely a creation of the 20th century. The land was agricultural for centuries before the comfortable semi-detached houses were built in the 1930s, which has meant that this large district has relatively few items of historical or architectural interest. Yet Childwall has an ancient inn, surprising links with *University Challenge* and Regent's Park, a fragment of Civil War history, and the oldest church in the city.

The village is old enough to be mentioned in Domesday as 'Cilduuelle', which shows that the name at the end of the 11th century was pronounced practically as it is today. Cilduuelle is in turn derived from the Old Norse phrase 'Kelda Vollr' or 'spring field', and the area was known for its clear wells until fairly recently. The heart of modern Childwall is still the old village, centred on the church of All Saints and the Childwall Abbey pub. It sits on the slopes of a prominent hill that once marked the high point of Childwall Heath, a wilderness of gorse and heather, which stretched across to what is now Wavertree. Derek Whale mentions a 'Celtic' burial mound discovered here, but other evidence for this is slight.

There are still roads in existence that once ran across the Heath, and connected the little village to the other hamlets of the district. Yates and Perry's map from the late 18th century shows unnamed lanes that correspond to modern roads. 'Childwall Priory Road' (perhaps known even then as the road to the Priory) is linked to 'Dunbabin Road', which in turn connects with Heathfield Road. This road commemorates a house which once stood here called Heathfield, but which came first, the house, the field or the road is uncertain. Score Lane was certainly in existence by the Middle Ages, and for many years was known as the portway, which could denote an even older origin. It possibly connected the mediaeval church at Childwall with the more important one at Walton.

All Saints' is the oldest church building in Liverpool, and assumed its present form at the end of the 16th century. It was an important local church before the Reformation, and the Norris family of Speke Hall had close links with the church and were buried here. Yet it might have been a religious site for far longer. The layout of the churchyard has led some archaeologists to speculate that it is Anglo-Saxon in origin, which might make the village well over 1,000 years old. Certainly

Childwall Valley Road under construction in June 1931, running towards open countryside.

by the Middle Ages the parish was very large, covering an area from Childwall to the Mersey at Garston. This indicates that the population was small and thinly spread, confirming that the land was mainly used for agriculture. There would probably have been a number of smaller hamlets scattered across the landscape during this time, which have since disappeared.

The field next to the graveyard is called Bloody Acre or Acrefield, and has never been built on. It is possible that this gory place-name remembers a skirmish during the Civil War of the 1640s, as in living memory a sword of the period and a cannonball have been dug up in gardens along Score Lane. On the other hand, Peter Howell Williams records a 'local tradition' that 'Bloody Acrefield was the scene of a skirmish between the new landowners and the adherents of the Church, following Henry VIII's dispossession of church land.'

It is certain that huge areas of south Liverpool were owned and farmed by the monks of Stanlawe Abbey before the Dissolution of the Monasteries in the mid-

1500s, and this ecclesiastical heritage left its mark on the landscape. There used to be three stone crosses very near to Childwall church, perhaps marking the roads from neighbouring hamlets such as Speke, and one lay broken for years in the fields along Score Lane before being reassembled in 1936. A large stone-lined well on the slopes, towards what is now the railway line, was for years called the Monks' Bath. Childwall Priory Road and the Childwall Abbey public house would seem to mark a memory of great religious houses in the area, but famously there was neither priory nor abbey at Childwall. The 'priory' was a farmhouse, possibly mediaeval, which stood near to the modern Fiveways junction and was demolished in the 1930s for the widening of Queens Drive; it had a Gothic façade added later in its life, which may have given it the nickname. The 'abbey' is supposed to have been a reference to the ecclesiastical style of the old Childwall Hall, but it is also possible that it refers to the fact that the monks of Stanlawe Abbey owned land in Childwall for many years; perhaps it was once known as 'the Abbey's inn'. The building is at least mediaeval in origin, and for many years was a hotel as well as an inn. In the early 20th century it was frequently used by actors, and Ellen Terry and Henry Irving have left their names scratched in the windows of the upstairs rooms.

The other major building in Childwall was Childwall Hall. The earliest references to this building are from the early 1700s, but this building was

demolished in 1780 and a new Hall designed by John Nash, the architect of Regent Street and Regent's Park in London, built on the site for the local landowner Bamber Gascoyne. (The television presenter Bamber Gascoigne once told Derek Whale that he was related to this family.) This building was itself demolished in the late 1940s when it was discovered that the fabric was too badly decayed to be restored. Childwall Woods was once the landscaped park surrounding the Hall, and it is possible therefore that the lodge house at the main entrance to the woods is also by John Nash. The site of the Hall was for many years a technical college, but in recent years has been taken over by Phil Redmond's Mersey TV company. One of the oldest villages in Liverpool therefore now houses one of the newest, the tele-village of 'Brookside', and the soap opera's petrol station and shops can be seen from the safety of the woods. Fragments of the Hall's Gothic style were still evident in the 1970s, when children in the area called one enclosed stretch of wall 'the Chapel', perhaps continuing the local tradition of appropriating but misunderstanding the Gothic buildings of the area.

Childwall has a long and surprising association with education. Apart from the technical college, which once occupied the Mersey TV campus, Bishop Eton Monastery on Woolton Road was built as a school in the middle years of the 19th century, with the intention of becoming 'the Eton of the North'. The chapel was

begun in 1851 by the renowned architect Augustus Pugin, and finished by his son Edward; it is an attractive and delightful building. Next door to Bishop Eton stands St Joseph's home, which was built by Augustus Pugin as a private house between 1845 and 1847. Further along Woolton Road stood the extensive grounds of Childwall County Primary School. The large school building was used as a hospital during World War Two, but fell to developers in the late 1980s; the site is now new housing, with a smaller and more practical school hidden within it.

Childwall is also home to Hope University College. For many years the College was known as the Liverpool Institute of Higher Education, which comprised St Katherine's College (known as 'St Kaths') and the college of Christ & Notre Dame, usually shortened to 'Christs'. The Institute specialised in teaching qualifications and generations of Liverpool teachers received their degrees through it, including Willy Russell, now more famous as a playwright. The oldest buildings were built in the 1930s in a tasteful copy in dark rich brick of an Oxbridge college, with a cloister around a small garden, and a quadrangle open to the fields beyond. Christs, across Taggart Avenue, was a 1960s development that has softened with time. The college buildings were designed by Weightman & Bullen, who built many good buildings in the city, and the chapel here is particularly attractive. The college has a long history in Liverpool; for many years the old Notre Dame had buildings on

Mount Pleasant, and Hope now has an additional site in the old school buildings of St Francis Xavier's in Everton.

Modern Childwall was laid out as a middle-class suburb from the 1930s onwards, as road links with the city improved. Landscapes designed for road transport can be dull and bland, but Childwall has over a thousand years of history, and the conservation area around the church and the Abbey Hotel has retained its rural atmosphere.

The Childwall Abbey Hotel, one of Liverpool's oldest inns.

Next page: Childwall Church and the Childwall Abbey Hotel.

Further reading

Liverpool City Council, *Buildings of Liverpool*, 1978.

Archive Training Unit, *Childwall*, 1986.

Liverpool City Libraries, *Childwall A Brief History*, 1985.

Peter Howell Williams, *Liverpolitana*, Liverpool, 1971.

Derek Whale, *Lost Villages of Liverpool* Part I, 1985.

George Yates and William Perry 'Map of Leverpool and Environs' 1768.

CHILDWALL
ABBEY

EDGE HILL

Edge Lane marks the edge of the old township of West Derby, but Edge Hill is probably named simply after the sharp descent towards Liverpool, and has been called Edge Hill only since the end of the 18th century. On maps from that time it is marked as Chetham's Brow, and the area around the church of St Mary is marked as the heart of the old village. The church was built in 1812 in a pretty 'Gothick' style, but the village is older and still has some handsome Georgian houses and shop fronts. Modern building around Holland Place and Marmaduke Street has been sympathetic and despite the ugliness of some of the surrounding 1960s development, Edge Hill retains a nominal village identity.

Edge Hill once overlooked the Mosslake, a huge expanse of water and boggy ground that separated the village from the swelling town of Liverpool. It was so large, and the ground so saturated, that for many years it was felt that it was a natural barrier to the city's expansion. The lines of Smithdown Lane and Mount Pleasant today are unnaturally kinked, showing where the bog forced the road builders to work around it. The Mosslake or Mosslake Fields stretched from

Hoardings on Mount Vernon and West Derby Streets in May 1930. This is now the grounds of the Royal Liverpool University Hospital.

Paddington and Brownlow Hill to Upper Parliament Street, and from Smithdown Lane to Hope Street. It was a feature of the Great Heath that covered much of what is today south Liverpool, from St George's Hall to Mossley Hill. During the winter the Mosslake was a sheet of water sometimes 280 acres in extent. 'A vast expanse of waste and bogland,' wrote Charles Hands. Mosslake Fields were finally drained in the early 19th century, and the first Liverpool Botanic Gardens was laid out. The old gardens are still commemorated by street names; they stood between Myrtle Street, Olive Street and Laurel Street, now Melville Place. The designer was William Roscoe, one of the giants of Liverpool history. In 1802, when they were laid out, the Botanic Gardens were in the countryside, but became a popular attraction for Liverpool people for over 30 years. In 1836 they moved to the south side of Edge Lane to what is now Botanic Park, and to Calderstones Park in the mid-20th century.

Edge Hill was for many years 'the place of residence of many of Liverpool's merchant princes', and until the 19th century the landscape was fields, woods and small farming hamlets. This pastoral landscape was also dotted with the bigger houses of Liverpool's wealthy; some built by the newly rich escaping the noise and smoke of Liverpool, and some long-established, the homes of local landowners. One of the oldest and largest houses was Vernon Hall, or Mount Vernon Hall. It stood on the corner of Edge Lane and Hall Lane, which was once literally the lane

Kinglake Street in November 1912, looking towards St Mary's church.

Oxford Street Circus in March 1909. To the right of the lamppost are Olive Street and modern Melville Place.

to the hall. It was possibly built in 1607 and an old tradition records it being used as the headquarters of the Parliamentarian general Thomas Fairfax during the Civil War. Liverpool's suburbs have many Civil War stories, from skirmishes in Childwall and Prince Rupert in Everton to Cromwell's men camping in the churchyard of the Ancient Chapel of Toxteth; certainly Vernon Hall was important enough to be inhabited by a succession of Liverpool worthies, now largely forgotten. Its age and size gave rise to rumours of hauntings; a later occupant described 'empty rooms which never seemed to be unoccupied and corridors which gave the feeling of having been vacated a moment before…' Vernon Hall was demolished in 1888, and was unfortunately never explored by architectural historians who could have determined its age.

The area was still rural when Tunnel Road was cut through the fields to give access to Edge Hill railway station. It is easy to forget the age of this station. It is still in use today and opened in 1836, when an earlier passenger station at Crown Street was found to be impractical and was turned to goods use. The strange station at Edge Hill was hollowed out of the hillside, and waiting rooms, ticket offices and workshops were cut from the solid rock. The station was connected to the depots at Crown Street and Wapping on the docks by tunnels, which were crowned by great chimneys in the form of Doric columns 100 feet high. They were dramatic enough to lead contemporary writers to call them 'the Pillars of Hercules', but existed to take fumes and smoke away from the winding engines that guided the trains down to the depots at Crown Street and Wapping, as these tunnels were too narrow for locomotives. The winding engines were themselves housed in an ornate 'Moorish Arch' which spanned the gorge, and through which the passenger trains ran to Broadgreen and Huyton and over the plain to Manchester. 'The whole area must have created a very favourable impression to travellers at the time,' wrote David Singleton in his book *Liverpool and Manchester Railway*, 'and must have been a scene of considerable activity.' This original Edge Hill station can now only be glimpsed from the later buildings, for an attempt in the 1970s and 1980s to build a visitor centre and attract tourists came to nothing.

The early railway workings are not the only tunnels in Edge Hill; perhaps today the area is even more famous for its unknown miles of tunnels burrowed in the early 19th century by Joseph Williamson, the 'Mole of Edge Hill.' Williamson was a tobacco merchant, and used the money he made from the business to build 'some of the most extraordinary operations that can be conceived,' in James Picton's words. Picton was writing in the 1870s, and he is unable to keep the exasperated astonishment out of his voice, despite the fact that many people would have

A tram turning from Oxford Street onto Grove Street in October 1910. Only the roads are still there today.

A splendid view of Grove Street near the junction with Oxford Street, taken in December 1938.

remembered Joseph Williamson. 'His manners were as eccentric as his conduct,' he wrote. 'Of noble exterior and courtly bearing when he chose to practise it, his usual costume was mean and slovenly, and his manner to strangers offensive.' Williamson settled in Mason Street in 1806, and retired in 1818 when he began to build. He filled up the vacant spaces between the houses on Mason Street with buildings 'of the strangest and most uncouth character,' according to Picton. 'Projections and recesses in irregular disorder, storeys of all heights, some rooms without windows, others apparently all window, some buildings run up by working day and night, others left unfinished for years…' It is a great pity that none of Williamson's strange and uncouth buildings survive today. He is chiefly remembered for the miles of tunnels he constructed beneath Edge Hill, supposedly to give work to soldiers returning from the Napoleonic Wars. The tunnels stretched for miles in all directions. 'The whole hillside became honeycombed, excavated and pervaded by caves, vaults and yawning chasms utterly without meaning, plan or object,' wrote

Asphalt laying on Tunnel Road in September 1949.

Picton. It is possible that his tunnelling almost bankrupted Williamson, as 'his means were considerably straitened later in life.' He died in 1841 and was buried in St Thomas's churchyard, on the corner of Paradise Street and Park Lane. The cemetery was cleared when the church was demolished in 1905, but Williamson was alone in not being moved; he lies there still, beneath the cars of the Anglican diocesan officials who use the old churchyard as a car park. This harmless eccentric and his 'whims and oddities' ruffled Picton's Victorian sensibilities. He describes the work as having a 'whimsical and misplaced ingenuity', of it all being forgotten 'like an uneasy nightmare', even that Williamson changed the character of the area for the worse. Yet fortunately this is far from the case. Today the Mole of Edge Hill is again famous in Liverpool, and attempts are being made to open at least some of his unknown miles of tunnels as a tourist attraction.

Edge Hill and Kensington were massively built up by the Victorians, with their familiar terraced streets of red-brick and terracotta

Kinglake Street and Holland Place on a sunny day in October 1950.

houses. The village was joined with Wavertree and with the city centre, as the old Mosslake Fields were built on. Some of the fine wide streets built here should have been saved, but the elegant townhouses of Upper Huskisson Street and Upper Canning Street were demolished in the 1960s, and the Falkner Estate built. In less than 20 years it had become derelict, and it too was demolished. The new Liverpool Women's Hospital stands there today. The smaller terraces of the Kinglake Street/Mason Street district were cleared in the 1950s and 1960s, and grim apartment blocks built. Many of these have in turn been cleared for smart modern houses. The old Georgian village centre has survived this upheaval, and is now a conservation area. Yet more could be done to enhance the appeal of this handsome terminus to busy Wavertree Road, with its shops and businesses. Edge Hill could become a popular urban village, especially since much of the totalitarian 1960s housing has been replaced by a student district built near Williamson's old home on Mason Street, and the Overbury Street area also has attractive new municipal housing.

Further reading

Charles Robert Hands, *The History of Edge Hill,* Liverpool, 1915.

James Picton, *Memorials of Liverpool,* Volume II, 1873.

David Singleton, *Liverpool and Manchester Railway*, Dalesman, 1975.

Derek Whale, *Lost Villages of Liverpool* Part II, 1985.

EVERTON

There is an excellent book, long out of print, which is the definitive guidebook to Everton's history. Robert Syers wrote *The History of Everton* in the 1830s, a time when the old agricultural ways of the village were being overturned by new housing and greater links with Liverpool. Syers was concerned that Everton's history would be lost, yet his enthusiasm in presenting the village as a rural Arcadia must only have made it more attractive to people seeking a home away from the smokes of Liverpool but within easy reach of it. Is it any coincidence that the first building developer of Everton was a man named George Syers? Yet Robert Syers's book is an interesting one, for Everton has a fine history. Despite being a small village for centuries it had an involvement in the war against the Spanish Armada and the English Civil War, it had a part in the early history of ballooning and in the eerie flights of Spring-heeled Jack. Liverpool's rich men built here in the 18th century and one of Britain's greatest theatre designers did so in the 20th; and today it is known all over the world because of an internationally-famous football club. Everton has become a general name for large chunks of north Liverpool, bordered by Scotland Road and Vauxhall on the riverside, by New Islington and West Derby Road on the city side, and perhaps by Oakfield Road to the north-east.

'It is probable that Everton at the time of the Roman invasion, and indeed long before that epoch, was a rude hamlet,' Syers wrote. Everton is the highest point on the long stone spine that runs through Liverpool parallel to the river, which he felt made an ideal location. The village would be well placed for local farming, some hunting and trapping in the immense forest of West Derby, and perhaps even some fishing in the river below. Derek Whale agreed about the good location, and remarks that the original village ran from the corner of Eastbourne Street, on the

brow, in a curved line to the corner of Breck Road. 'Farmland lay about it,' he wrote, 'and in summer, this was one of the fairest villages of Merseyside...'

The village was known as Evreton in 1094, and Euerton in 1201, and has been Everton since the later 13th century, by which time it was a distinct township. It was not part of the manor of West Derby, as the inhabitants held their lands by yearly rent and service to the king, but it was clearly a small manor, mentioned in many documents as being passed from one owner to another very easily. For many centuries the village was a small cluster of houses along Village Street and Everton Brow, which is now once again surrounded by fields. The surrounding land was not very fertile, however, and was mainly used for pasture. Villagers of Kirkdale paid

A busy scene in 1913 outside the necropolis, West Derby Road, which is being demolished to be replaced with Grants Gardens. The misty spire belongs to Emmanuel Church which stood on the corner of Boaler Street.

A traction engine towing a trailer of prefabricated concrete walls, a revolutionary building method when this picture was taken in Everton in October 1904.

the 'Evertonians' a rent to pasture their cattle on the fields of Everton. The larger village of Kirkdale had more fertile land than Everton up on the hill, and for this reason Syers describes it as 'the garden of Liverpool'.

The oldest landmark in Everton was the Beacon, which stood on the highest point of the ridge where St George's church now stands, at the end of Beacon Lane. Syers believed that the Beacon was erected during the 1580s, at a time when the Spanish Armada threatened England, although earlier writers dated it to possibly the 1220s. It was visited 'on a fine afternoon' in December 1802, by 'two persons fond of exploring ancient structures.' They commented that the Beacon was a plain, square, stone edifice two storeys in height, with a kitchen area downstairs and a guardroom upstairs. The views from the top on a clear day must have been magnificent, and the two antiquarians found 'many initials, and indeed full length names, were chiselled; but none of celebrity.'

During the Civil War, the Royalist general Prince Rupert brought his troops here to retake Liverpool, then held by defiant Parliamentarians, for the Crown. It is

The old Cloth Market on Fox Street in 1905, the site of Richmond Fair. This was cleared five years later for the building of St Mary of the Angels' church.

probable that he chose to quarter his troops in Everton because of the excellent views of Liverpool. His famous and disparaging quote on Liverpool 'T'is but a crow's nest a parcel of boys could take' was possibly made after surveying the town from the Beacon. Rupert chose a comfortable cottage for himself, and his officers were quartered in other local homes. His men, however, pitched tents on the heath behind the village, and the Old Campfield, one of the few buildings on modern Heyworth Street, remembers their camp. The pub is still decorated by a faded 1970s painting of a suitably cavalier Prince Rupert. Everton was a Royalist stronghold at this time, for the village was also home to priests expelled from Liverpool for their loyalty to the Crown. These exiled priests performed marriages in the Beacon and perhaps funerals, for during the excavations for the foundations of St George's two bodies were discovered, dated by their clothes and accoutrements to the 1640s.

Prince Rupert's engineers built a battery on a natural prominence just below the cottage, but this was found to be too far from the town for his guns; further trenches and gun emplacements were discovered on modern Commutation Row in the 19th century. The battery in Everton revealed a gun and sword 'thickly encrusted with rust' during building work in the 1840s, at the same time that Prince Rupert's cottage was demolished.

Anthony Street from Beatrice Street in 1948, with some boys making use of the cleared site to play cricket.

The Beacon was blown down in a severe storm in 1803, but was very probably visited by Thomas De Quincey, who stayed in Liverpool as a young man. The Romantic writer, author of *Confessions of an English Opium-Eater*, was first here in 1801 at the age of 16. He stayed with his mother in a cottage in Middle Lane, later renamed Everton Terrace. De Quincey was befriended by the Liverpool banker William Clarke, and through him met William Roscoe, the biographer Dr Currie, and the Unitarian minister Dr Shepherd, who formed a literary and political group known as the Liverpool Literary Coterie or, less favourably, the Liverpool Jacobins

for their support of the aims of the French Revolution. In later life, De Quincey published his literary memoirs and was famously rather scathing of the group, which made him few friends in Liverpool. He also witnessed one of the biggest fires that the port had ever seen, when some cotton warehouses in Goree Piazza caught fire in 1802. De Quincey recorded the fact that some of the sparks flew as far as Warrington, so he probably didn't have to stray far from Middle Lane to see it.

Many 18th-century Liverpool fortunes were made in the Caribbean, whether from slavery, sugar or molasses, and many of the new rich built property in Everton, knocking down cottages two and three hundred years old in order to do so. But the air was healthier than in Liverpool, and from the heights they could see their ships entering and leaving the port, so very old cottages like the Throstle's Nest on the top of the hill had to be demolished. The Coffee House tavern at the foot of Rupert Lane and Everton Village served as an 'assembly rooms' for the little community of rich men, and the names of their estates still sound across the years; 'St Domingo' was an estate commemorating a naval skirmish off that Caribbean island, 'Bronte' – long a famous pub in Everton valley – was named after Lord Nelson's Sicilian estate by a man who had made a fortune as his wine merchant. The merchants are remembered in street names too – Plumpton, Woodhouse, Gregson. The newly wealthy were attracted by the village's location and much-improved communications with Liverpool. How far the roads had improved is shown by the fact that 70,000 people came to Everton in the summer of 1812 to watch an ascent by the famous balloonist James Sadler, which surely could not have been possible over poor roads. Everton was becoming popular with day visitors and in 1787 the famous lock-up was built to accommodate drunks overnight, at the same time and for the same reason as the lock-up in Wavertree. The little port was flexing its muscles and creeping nearer, but Robert Syers could still describe Everton in the 1830s as 'a delectable spot indeed and almost entitled to the denomination of a modern Arcadia.'

A jumble of ashpits on Nursery Street in 1908, showing how cramped these houses were.

The Victorians transformed Everton from a fashionable rural village into a suburb of their new city. The fields disappeared under miles of terraced streets built mainly by the Welsh, who dominated the building trade at this time. They arrived in such huge numbers that Welsh newspapers and advertisements were printed in Kirkdale and Everton, and the district had Welsh chapels of many denominations. The Irish too came to Liverpool in their tens of thousands, especially after the notorious Famine of the 1840s. They found work on the docks and in the workshops of Vauxhall, but brought their religious divisions with them; by and large the Irish Catholics lived on Scotland Road, and the Protestant Orangemen lived around Netherfield Road, until this sectarianism was forcibly dispersed in the 1960s and 1970s. Their surviving churches are among Everton's most attractive buildings; the odd church of St Polycarp on Netherfield Road, once fiercely Orange and now a workshop; the famous St Anthony's on Scotland Road, strangely modern yet built 170 years ago; and the dark spike of St Francis Xavier's, its sooty sandstone hiding a golden Gothic interior, where poet-and-priest Gerard Manley Hopkins used to say Mass.

The Victorians also brought their bogeymen to Everton, and the spire of St Francis Xavier's was once clawed by Spring-heeled Jack. Draped in a black cloak,

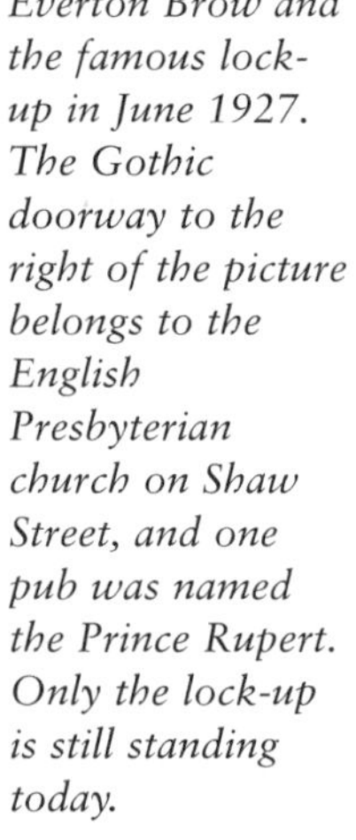

Everton Brow and the famous lock-up in June 1927. The Gothic doorway to the right of the picture belongs to the English Presbyterian church on Shaw Street, and one pub was named the Prince Rupert. Only the lock-up is still standing today.

his eyes flashing and blue flames spouting from his mouth, Jack terrorised people – especially women – on many occasions, before bounding away, leaping incredible distances to escape. Most of his appearances were in London, but Jack also appeared in Liverpool. He was seen on High Park Street in the 1880s, and Richard Whittington-Egan records two visits to Everton by this strange and threatening figure. He was seen in Shaw Street in 1888, when he is supposed to have leaped to the top of the church spire, and 16 years later, in what was possibly his last-ever appearance, he was seen bounding across William Henry Street by 'hundreds' of people.

Perhaps some of Jack's awe-struck audience also heard William Gladstone speak in Hengler's Circus on Everton Road. The great Victorian politician had close links with Liverpool, and spoke in the showground of Hengler's Circus on at least two occasions. In

The old and the new on a rainy day in October 1952. This is the corner of Virgil and Cazneau Streets.

The new Everton – a housing model from 1958.

1895 he held a full house (well over 4,000 people) spellbound by 'a great oration' on the political situation in the Balkans, which was seen by William Forwood. He vividly recalled the 'perfect torrent of eloquence' 15 years later when he wrote *Recollections of a Busy Life*, which has many off-the-cuff memories of 19th-century Liverpool. On another occasion Gladstone spoke on Irish Home Rule. He believed so passionately in his subject, as no doubt did many of his audience, that he spoke without notes for up to five hours.

Everton at the end of the 19th century was at the height of its population and

importance, but many of the houses were slums, and overcrowding and poverty were endemic. The poverty and squalor endured by many people living in the district at this time has been well documented, on an almost street-by-street basis, by Freddy O'Connor, in his book *Liverpool Our City Our Heritage*. The 20th century saw great changes, but Robert Syers would find little that was delectable or Arcadian about modern Everton. It is one of the poorest districts of modern

Two sunny views of the Braddocks, multi-storey flats in Everton, in 1959.

Liverpool and has been shamefully treated by successive generations of city planners, who in many cases demolished what was good and built badly. The 1960s and 1970s saw the demolition of many miles of Everton streets, by no means all of them slums. The fine Victorian houses at the top of Everton Hill were demolished and eventually replaced by the soulless Everton Park, a strangely useless and vainglorious piece of urban landscaping. The replacement housing was in many cases itself demolished after only 20 years, and the survivors seem mean-spirited and cheap.

Yet the district does have some good points. The oldest building in modern Everton is St George's Church, designed by the iron church master Thomas Rickman and built in 1815 on the site of the Beacon. Together with Everton Library and the Mere public house the church forms the centre of a small collection of buildings that are an attractive heart to the modern 'village'. Brougham Terrace, associated as the city's registry office with births, marriages and deaths, also had the earliest Mosque in the country and was designed by James Picton, the Liverpool

Old Everton – Prince Edwin Street in 1920. All of this property was cleared after 1945. With new houses on it, the street now runs alongside Everton Park.

A fine view of Everton lock-up and Browside in 1927, looking towards the Anne Fowler Memorial Home.

Smoky Everton rooftops in June 1927.

Huge tower blocks being built in the Garibaldi Street area, off Netherfield Road, in November 1960.

Eastbourne Street in October 1932, near the heart of old Everton village. All these houses were cleared after World War Two.

L.BARKER
JACOB'S CREAM CRACKERS
RED SEAL TOFFEE
RED SEAL TOFFEE
GENERAL L.BARKER STORES
HOME MADE ICES
HOME MADE ICES
ICES

historian. Grants Gardens opposite is the site of the city's first necropolis, a purpose-built cemetery dating from the 1820s and for many years (due to its proximity to the registry office) a strange choice for wedding photographs. And down West Derby Road is the huge and gloriously ornate Locarno ballroom and theatre, designed by the great Edwardian theatre-designer Frank Matcham, and now enjoying a renaissance as a theatre and sports venue. Everton also has the huge water tower that in the 1850s formed part of the first coherent attempt to bring fresh water to the city, and which reminded Quentin Hughes of Piranesi's etchings of Rome.

And Everton still has the geographical strengths it has always had. It has good air and views across the city to the Wirral and the Welsh hills, easy access to the city centre and the north and east of Liverpool. Some urban regeneration has begun. Very little of the new private money currently associated with fashionable city living has yet found its way to the north end of the city, but the old Collegiate school building (designed in the 1840s by

Everton Library and community centre, one of the few buildings of any age surviving in modern Everton.

Previous page: A famous view of Netherfield Road in 1927.

The pretty Mere public house, opposite Everton Library.

St George's, the oldest of Thomas Rickman's iron churches, on the site of the Beacon in Everton.

Harvey Lonsdale Elmes) is being rejuvenated as modern apartments, as is the old Baptist chapel next door. Many of the elegant Georgian houses on Shaw Street are being renovated. Liverpool Hope University College has revived the other school buildings around the church of St Francis Xavier, and given the old church a new lease of life. The city authorities have been slow to respond, but have built some good small houses on Prince Edwin Street and towards Islington. Much more needs to be done, but the very fact that so much is derelict and valueless means that Everton is a clean slate; fine new housing should be built celebrating the sense of community, the district's history, the good location. Why shouldn't Everton become Liverpool's first garden suburb of the 21st century, an elegant and desirable place to live and work?

Further reading

James Picton, *Memorials of Liverpool*, Volume II, Liverpool, 1873. Robert Syers, *The History of Everton*, Liverpool, 1830. Freddy O'Connor, *Liverpool Our City Our Heritage*, Liverpool, 1990.

The gigantic Water Tower in Everton, built between 1854 and 1857 by Thomas Duncan, Liverpool Corporation's first water engineer.

GATEACRE, BELLE VALE AND NETHERLEY

Gateacre

Gateacre is not one of Liverpool's 'lost villages'. The heart of the district is surrounded today by modern housing which swept around it in huge waves in the middle years of the 20th century, but the old centre was left intact. The place-name is derived from 'gate' meaning road or way, and 'acre', meaning field, indicating perhaps a hamlet on the road to pasture. The word is Middle English, which means that it was named seven or eight hundred years ago, although its nearness to Woolton also gave it the name Little Woolton. There is nothing in the village today older than the 17th century, but Gateacre has kept its rural atmosphere. Its heart is still the village green and the roads connecting Gateacre with Childwall, Woolton and Garston. The village has attractive rows of sandstone houses with walls of weathered stone, and neat cottages with slate roofs. The most obvious building materials are brick and the local red sandstone, apart from the black and white half-

Lee Hall in March 1956, not long before demolition.

A quiet Gateacre Village in January 1952.

Prefabricated houses on Lineside Road in August 1953. These were built to house people made homeless during the recent war.

timbered look favoured by the Victorians. The names of Gateacre's old inns reflect the farming traditions of the area; Black Bull, Brown Cow, Bear & Staff. The pubs are quite old by Liverpool standards; the Black Bull and the Bear & Staff are originally 18th-century, while the Brown Cow was built from two 19th-century cottages knocked together. Despite the unrelenting traffic, the village green seems surrounded by tall trees, and there is still woodland opposite the Bear & Staff and over towards the old railway, now an urbanised country walk.

Gateacre has one of the oldest churches in the city; the attractive Unitarian Chapel built in 1700. The rambling Gateacre Hall on Halewood Road was built in the 17th century and added to over the years, so that it now has extra doors and porches, strange chimneys, and probably more windows than rooms. It also has the

A children's playground on Lineside Road in 1954.

Slave Gate, a gate made of wrought iron taken from the site now occupied by Tower Building, on the Strand and Water Street in the city centre. Despite the slave trade's importance to the city comparatively few slaves passed through Liverpool, and so it is unlikely that the building that the Gate came from was really a holding centre for slaves, but the name has stuck.

Belle Vale and Netherley

Modern Gateacre is surrounded by huge housing developments, mainly built in the latter half of the 20th century. At the end of Childwall Valley Road the city ends abruptly, and the houses look out onto farmland and woods. These estates of Netherley and Belle Vale were purpose-built exercises in suburban planning, and Netherley in particular has had to be drastically altered from the original plans. The ugly six-storey apartment blocks of the 1960s, connected above ground by concrete tunnels, have been demolished and replaced by roads of bungalows and gardens, less adventurous but safer and on a more human scale.

Belle Vale is an older district that was centred on Belle Vale Hall and a small hamlet called Throstle Nest, on Belle Vale Road near the Victorian St Stephen's church. The hamlet has long since disappeared under the 1950s estate of Lee Park. This was an 18th-century estate, with a tall brick house of 1773 described in 1955 as 'one of the most perfect of smaller Georgian houses in Lancashire.' The modern Belle Vale radiates from a large and popular shopping centre and baths, built as the centre of a new suburb. Belle Vale was more successful than its neighbour Netherley, perhaps because it had less lofty aims and built streets of small houses from the beginning, but the only building of any interest is the Church of Our Lady of the Assumption, built in 1949 and still striking today.

Further reading
Peter Fleetwood-Hesketh, *Murray's Guide to Lancashire,* 1955.
Derek Whale, *Lost Villages of Liverpool,* Part II, 1985

KENSINGTON AND FAIRFIELD

Kensington

The Liverpool district of Kensington takes its name from the road connecting Low Hill with Prescot Road, the important coach road out through Old Swan to Prescot. It was named Kensington in 1804, before which it was called Prescot Lane. Sir William Forwood, mayor of the new city in 1880 and again in 1903, remembered growing up here in the 1840s. 'My father's house at Edge Hill overlooked the grounds of Mount Vernon Hall and the gardens of the vicarage [of St Mary's]; to the east were open fields, with a few large villas dotted about.' He also described

Sacred Heart Church, Hall Lane, on a gloomy February day in 1949.

Sun Hall, Kensington, 1956. This grand hall was demolished soon afterwards.

the area as 'a very charming and attractive suburb' and remembered a landscape of villas surrounded by large gardens, the houses 'large and handsome'.

One of the attractive houses had been built by Dr Solomon. He began medical practice in Marybone, off Tithebarn Street, before moving to Brownlow Hill in about 1800. At the end of the 18th century he developed the 'Balm of Gilead', a tonic and pick-me-up. The little bottles sold in their thousands and made Solomon a rich man, and 'one of the institutions of Liverpool', according to James Picton. In 1804 he built himself Gilead House in Kensington, and the house soon became famous for the beauty and fragrance of its gardens. They were one of the first sights of Liverpool that travellers on the stage coaches saw as they drove in from Old Swan. Dr Solomon died in 1819 and was buried in a mausoleum in Aigburth, now lost beneath an unremarkable street called Cooper Avenue South; but before the development of this area, 'Solomon's Vaults' was a local footpath.

The open land between Liverpool and the select semi-rural suburb of Fairfield

The busy workshop of the Corporation's passenger transport depot on Edge Lane in June 1960.

was known as Kensington Fields from the early 19th century, and was a landscape of fields dotted with large houses. Towards the end of the century the land began to be built up with streets of red-brick terraced housing, and as early as 1846 Kensington Fields became the site of a reservoir built to

The ornate carving of Christ Church, Kensington, built in 1871.

bring fresh water from Rivington Pike into the rapidly expanding town. As the town grew, the old coaching route was built up and the country villas demolished. Solomon's presence in the area was remembered in Balm Street and Gilead Street, built near the site of his villa and famous gardens. Many streets were named after Queen Victoria's German in-laws and family; Leopold, Bathenburg, and Guelph Streets, Albert and Adelaide Streets, and finally Jubilee Drive, laid out in 1888 and named to celebrate Victoria's 50 years as Queen and Empress in 1887. Jubilee Drive runs alongside the old Kensington Fields reservoir, which was acquired by the city authorities at this time and laid out with borders and pathways as Kensington

Edge Lane near the Botanic Gardens on a misty day in October 1912.

Hoardings on the corner of Rawlins Street and Prescot Road, May 1930.

'Here the weary are at rest' – the old Jewish cemetery on Deane Road.

Gardens. Strange to think, but Kensington was almost a 'new town' at this time: it had an elegant public library, fine public gardens, imposing churches, and streets of new houses with good access to the city's offices.

In 1955, Percy Phillips converted one of these Victorian houses, 38 Kensington, into a recording studio. Among the many local musicians who recorded there were the Quarrymen, then comprising John Lennon, Paul McCartney, George Harrison, John Lowe and Colin Hanton. In 1958 they recorded a number of standards and *In Spite Of All the Danger*, a new composition by Harrison and McCartney. This very early recording in the history of the Beatles survives, and was released as part of Apple/EMI's *Beatles Anthology* in 1995.

Kensington is one of the poorest areas of the city and has little in common with its London namesake, but it does have some interesting buildings. The most striking are the imposing Christ Church, built in 1867, and the library next door, which dates from 1890. It was designed by the City Architect, Thomas Shelmerdine, who designed other city libraries in a similar style. On Deane Road, Kensington also has one of the lost Jewish cemeteries of the city. Charles Hands saw the cemetery in its prime and described it as 'ornamental, beautifully laid out, well-kept… The entrance is by a chaste portico in pure classic stone which bears the Hebrew inscription 'here the weary are at rest''. Today the cemetery is closed and abandoned and trees obscure the entrance from Deane Road.

Kensington is one of the most run-down and neglected districts of Liverpool, but at the time of writing, it is possible that it will be regenerated by local groups and the city council. Plans have been announced to demolish much of the substandard and undesirable terraced housing and replace it with modern houses with gardens and small driveways, as has been done successfully in the south of the city.

The newly restored Kensington Library.

Fairfield

Fairfield takes its name from the Fairfield estate, which lay along Prescot Road. Edward Falkner, who laid out the Falkner estate in Toxteth, bought it in the 18th century and built himself a house, which was rapidly nicknamed Teacaddy Hall from its appearance. The district was farmland for many years, with villas and large farmhouses standing in their own grounds, but the following century saw these farms and small estates built up as the new city of Liverpool needed housing.

At first the rich built large villas on wide streets, but soon the developers saw Fairfield's potential and the district was laid out with long streets of housing. The country lanes of Prescot Road and Kensington became one of the most important routes into the city from the new suburbs of Old Swan and Fairfield. Today Fairfield has lost much of its 'rural suburb' identity, but in Prospect Vale and Elm Park, Laurel Road and around the curious church of St John the Divine, Fairfield has kept many of its wide roads, sandstone walls and handsome early Victorian property.

Ornate iron grille, Low Hill post office. Kensington has many fine, if overlooked, buildings.

Further reading

William Forwood, *Recollections of a Busy Life,* Liverpool, 1910.

Charles Hands, *The History of Edge Hill,* Liverpool, 1915.

James Picton, *Memorials of Liverpool* Volume II, Liverpool, 1873.

KIRKDALE

Kirkdale has always been defined by roads, and its links with other places. It straddles the point where the roads from Bootle and the heights of Everton meet Scotland Road, and is strung out along Stanley Road and Walton Road running through to Walton. These roads have been in existence for centuries, and it was their importance that established Kirkdale; although essentially a Victorian suburb it has an old village core, and a history stretching back to the Domesday Book.

Kirkdale is a Norse name, meaning 'the low ground on which stood the church', although it is also possible that the name implies 'the low ground on the way to the church', and could have been the route from Liverpool to its church at Walton. The Norman tax-assessors wrote down the village's assets for the Domesday Book of 1086 and called the village 'Chirchedele', but it was 'Kirkedale' by 1185, and 'Kierkedale' in a document written 15 years later, so the place-name has been in use for at least 800 or 1,000 years. Chirkdale Street is an echo of older spellings for the district. In its prime Kirkdale was a large village, with connections with Everton, Bootle and Walton, and the important road into Liverpool.

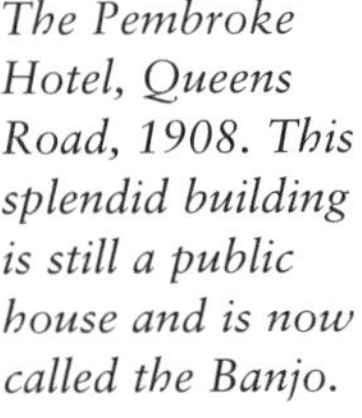

The Pembroke Hotel, Queens Road, 1908. This splendid building is still a public house and is now called the Banjo.

Reading Street, off Stanley Road, on a wash day in May 1936.

James Picton was able to trace the 'dale' itself, since he was writing in the 1870s at a time when houses had not completely obliterated the geography of the area. He records two low hills with a shallow valley between them, one now built over by Blackfield Terrace on Stanley Road and the other on the site of the Industrial Schools near to the old gaol. The stream running between these hills rose in Walton and joined the Mersey at the site of Canada Dock.

Early in the 13th century Kirkdale became one of the possessions and the chief seat of the Moore family, who had settled in Liverpool 100 years earlier. The Moores were important in Liverpool's civic life for 20 generations, representing the town in Parliament and active as local landowners. They lived in Bank Hall, which stood between the village and the river, on the corner of Bankhall Lane and

88

Bankhall Street near Sandhills station. (Many people in modern Liverpool would not consider this Kirkdale at all, but rather Vauxhall or Sandhills; the boundaries have shifted over the centuries as Kirkdale's shoreline has been built up.) The most interesting family member was Colonel John Moore, who lived in the mid-17th century and who seems to have made the most of his social position and wealth. The family were fiercely Parliamentarian during the Civil War, but John Moore was no Puritan. His household was described as 'hell upon earth', but the Victorian histories will only say that 'his personal character does not seem to have been of the consistently moral type associated with the designation of Puritan.' Colonel John Moore fought against Prince Rupert during the bloody skirmishes for Liverpool, and after Parliament's ultimate victory was one of the regicides, the signatories to the death warrant of Charles I. Their family connections saved the Moores from utter ruin at the Restoration of the Monarchy in 1660, and John's son Edward wrote the famous Moore Rental, a business account of his property and land, at the end of the century; this is an invaluable source of information for local historians. The family lost their wealth and power in the early 18th century, and are today remembered in Oldhall Street – the site of an older Moore property – in Moorfields, once an area of their land, and in Bank Hall Station.

Bank Hall itself was demolished in about 1773, by which time Kirkdale was a large village on the main stagecoach road out of Liverpool, through Walton to

Tetlow Street in 1956, before clearance.

Stanley Road with prefabs, near Hermia Street, July 1950.

Prescot and Ormskirk. It was this road that caused the growth and survival of Kirkdale and ultimately its incorporation into the city of Liverpool. The road is marked on Yates & Perry's map of 1768 as Bevington Bush, now Scotland Road and Kirkdale Road, and it joined Netherfield Lane before becoming Walton Road on the other side of Kirkdale village. Although not named, Walton Breck Road ran down from 'Ann Field' to join Walton Lane, which ran through the fields to the smaller hamlet of Mare Green on the site of Stanley Park. Kirkdale was also connected to Bootle by 'Field Lane', now Westminster Road. All these roads were rural; at the time Kirkdale was a large village, which in modern terms stretched from the junction of Scotland Road and Netherfield Road to Barlow Lane, and down to Stanley Road, although the village also had undeveloped land down to the river.

In the century following the demolition of Bank Hall, these sandy hills were built over by Liverpool's expanding dock and warehouse system. The village was transformed by the expansion of the city's industries in the 19th century, and the building of the gaol in the early 1820s also enhanced the area's prosperity. For 70 years it attracted huge crowds of people to watch public executions, with local hotels being full of people awaiting an execution, and boatloads of day-trippers from Liverpool in the village to watch the fun. The gaol was bought by the Corporation in 1891, and demolished.

Ceres Street, off Brasenose Road, in 1954. The footbridge crosses the Leeds–Liverpool Canal.

Kirkdale's population also exploded as a result of the hundreds of thousands of Irish people left homeless and starving by the Great Famine, and who came to Liverpool and settled in Vauxhall, Kirkdale and Scotland Road. There was work in the new workshops and warehouses along the docks, railway and canal, but housing conditions were atrocious and Derek Whale comments that by 1871 slum-ridden Kirkdale was the most densely populated area of the city. The *Victoria History of Lancashire*, published in 1907, described the district as 'a mass of

Old cottages on Barlow Lane, Kirkdale.

The doorway to apartments over shops on Westminster Road, part of Kirkdale's all-too-often ignored Victorian heritage.

buildings, chiefly small cottage property, the dwellings of the working classes, mixed up with factories and warehouses, railways and shops. There are no natural features left, scarcely a green tree to relieve the monotony of ugly buildings and gloomy surroundings...' Much of the gloom of the district has gone with the industry and the coal fires, but waves of bright new ideas in city planning have left their mark on Kirkdale, and it is not a pretty district of the city. It is busy and bustling, especially along the main roads of Walton Road and Scotland Road, but unfortunate 1960s housing built to replace the slums has in many cases quickly deteriorated and been vandalised. Yet there is much of interest in this vibrant and bustling district today; rows of pretty cottages on Barlow Lane, attractive Victorian pub and shop fronts of red brick and terracotta, and green open spaces on West-

minster Road. Kirkdale is not a smart district, but it has vitality and energy that other areas lack perhaps because of its good position at the junction of ancient roads, busier and more important now than they have ever been.

Further reading

James Baines, *History, Directory, and Gazetteer of the of the County Palatine of Lancashire,* 1824–25, reprinted 1968.

James Picton, *Memorials of Liverpool* Volume II, Liverpool, 1873.

Stanley Rogers, *The Ancient Village of Kirkdale and Its Modern Developments,* Liverpool, 1912.

Victoria History of Lancashire Volume III,1907.

Derek Whale, *Lost Villages of Liverpool* Part III, 1985.

Kirkdale Victoriana – the fantastically ornate Liver Bird on the Old Bill, once a Fire and Police Station, on Westminster Road.

Rich Victorian carving on the Grand National public house, Westminster Road.

OLD SWAN

Broadgreen, Tuebrook, Stoneycroft, Knotty Ash and Thingwall

Old Swan

Until the 19th century many of the roads in this part of Liverpool were farm tracks connecting small hamlets, which had grown up at crossroads or near big houses. Old Swan sits at the centre of a patchwork of smaller districts that grew up in this way. Most still have a solid Victorian feel to them, with sandstone Gothic churches and streets of red-brick terraced houses. Old Swan itself is named after a public house, which stood on the corner of Broadgreen Road and Prescot Road on the site of the present Red House pub. The junction was a busy one, as it still is today. The

A tram bound for the Pier Head on Edge Lane Drive in October 1914. On these older trams, the crew worked outside in all weathers.

inn took its name, the Three Swans, from the coat-of-arms of the Walton family, who owned land in the area. The inn was a day's journey from Liverpool by stagecoach, and as the traffic to and from Liverpool increased, so did the prosperity of the village. It was also on the packhorse trail from Edge Hill that ran along Edge Lane and over Old Swan Hill towards Prescot, which was discovered beneath Edge Lane at the turn of the 20th century. It was a narrow trail, used for horses only, and 'much worn with the shoes on the horses.' As recently as the mid-18th century, packhorses carried much of the merchandise inland from the Lancashire ports, and the last packhorse owner in south Lancashire lived in Old Swan. His stables held a hundred animals.

As the village's prosperity increased, two further inns were built, and the three inns became known locally as the Old Swan, the Middle Swan and the Lower Swan. The Cygnet, on the corner of Derby Lane, maintains this tradition, and is an attractive

The handsome Barclay's bank, Old Swan.

St Oswald's church spire, Old Swan, erected in 1842 by Augustus Pugin, and possibly the first Catholic spire built in the north of England after the Reformation.

public house in the Art Deco style. The present Old Swan public house was built in about 1775 and so is probably the oldest building in the district, but Old Swan has a few interesting and attractive buildings. Augustus Welby Northmore Pugin, the greatest architect of the Victorian Gothic Revival, designed St Oswald's Church in 1842. Much of the building was rebuilt in the 1950s, but the spire, said to be the first Catholic spire in the north of England built since the Reformation, is still one of the landmarks of the district. The old Barclays Bank building, designed in the early 20th century by Grayson & Ould, is an attractive termination to St Oswald Street and was described by architectural historian Quentin Hughes as 'classical in style with brick and stone dressings and a Dutch gable'. And 'the Swan' has miles of good quality Victorian housing, from the red-brick terracing surrounding the centre to the elegant country houses built on Olive Mount, Liverpool's Mount of Olives, a small district named after an 18th-century villa. It has given its name to the deep railway gorge originally cut by the workmen of the Liverpool & Manchester Railway, and still in use today.

Broadgreen

The small hamlets of Broadgreen and Oak Vale have disappeared, swallowed by the enormous Edge Lane Drive. Broadgreen is famous today for its hospital, an important centre for the treatment of heart complaints. Oak Vale has not survived as a district, although a church at the bottom of Broadgreen Road has kept the name alive. Oak Hill Park in Oak Vale was once famous for the trees that were transplanted from the Ladies Walk. This was an 18th-century promenade on modern Leeds Street, which was cleared for the building of the Leeds–Liverpool Canal; the trees were uprooted and replanted in Oak Vale. The ground here must have been quite fertile, for this was once the site of a nursery owned and run by the Cunningham family. They exported tens of thousands of apple, pear, raspberry and gooseberry trees to the Americas in the early 19th century, and George Cunningham was one of the first to import the scarlet dahlia to this country. When the Liverpool & Manchester Railway was cut through his nursery in the 1830s, Cunningham

Cottages opposite the Rocket pub on Broad Green Road in March 1914, when Broad Green was still rural.

Broad Green Road and the Rocket pub in 1928, now the site of the road linking Edge Lane Drive with the motorway.

Queens Drive at Broad Green in 1928, crossing the railway line near the Rocket pub.

New houses on Rocky Lane, photographed on a sunny day in April 1936.

The main entrance of the Seamen's Orphanage, showing Alfred Waterhouse's love of solid Gothic detail.

smothered his bridge across the line with these rich, voluptuous flowers – but whether in celebration or protest is not recorded.

Broadgreen was a hamlet that grew up between the present day Gardener's Arms and the Rocket pub, but the hamlet has largely been replaced in the city's consciousness with 'the Rocket', the deafening network of roads that forms one of the gateways to the city, and links the beginning or end of the M57 with Queens Drive, the city's inner ring road. The junction is named after the Rocket pub, the latest of which was built in the late 1980s as the new roads were finalised. The first 'Rocket' was an inn built in the 1730s, which served Stephenson's men during the building of the Liverpool & Manchester Railway a hundred years later.

Tuebrook

Tuebrook is placed between Anfield and Newsham Park, and is today a largely undistinguished Victorian district. The name commemorates one of the lost rivers of the city, the Tew Brook, which rose on Edge Lane at a place called Springfield. The brook is marked on maps from the late 18th century, where it is depicted

A suitably bright day on Sunlight Street in September 1909.

Muirhead Avenue from the air, April 1924.

flowing roughly parallel to Green Lane, crossing West Derby Road (then called Tewbrook Lane) and Townsend Lane and flowing through the grounds of Walton Hall. It shadowed Rice Lane before heading into Fazakerley and joining the Alt. It is possible that the prefix Tue or Tew marks the brook as sacred at one time to the Norse god who has given his name to Tuesday, which might indicate a Viking presence in the area. For many centuries the brook flowed through a landscape of fields and woods, and when the antiquarian and topographer James Hoult published a history of this area in the late 1930s there were still old people who remembered Tuebrook and Stoneycroft as rural areas. Hoult played on the banks of the little river when he was a boy and remembered it flowing over Prescot Road, forcing the carts and wagons to use a ford.

The oldest building in Tuebrook is Tuebrook House, a solid farm building built in 1615. The building is still inhabited and is situated on West Derby Road. Architectural historian Quentin Hughes has described Tuebrook House as 'a charming example of the period well maintained.' The house was never moated or

Preparations for war – air-raid shelters on Brainerd Street in March 1940. In the background is the Seamen's Orphanage in Newsham Park.

fortified, and was therefore built at a time of relative security.

On the Yates & Perry map of 1768, 'Tewbrook' is a small hamlet clustered around the crossroads of Green Lane and Tew Brook Lane, modern West Derby Road. Green Lane is named, and carries on across the junction roughly along the line of Lisburn Lane. Stoneycroft, although not mentioned by name, is a similar smattering of farm buildings and wayside inns along Green Lane, which has therefore had this name for at least 240 years. It is not impossible that it has had the name and been in existence for far longer. 'Green lanes' were unmetalled roads, sometimes of prehistoric origin, and it would not be surprising to find one following the flat ground alongside a small river.

Modern Tuebrook is a creation of the Victorians, who built mile upon mile of terraces of neat red-brick houses to accommodate city workers. The area was well sited, with access to the city along West Derby Road and the amenities of Old Swan close at hand. It is worth remembering that Tuebrook would have been

The interior of the Brainerd Street air-raid shelter, March 1940.

on the edge of Liverpool when it was developed, with farmland beginning on modern Queens Drive and the rural village of West Derby an afternoon's walk away. The Victorians also laid out Newsham Park on the site of an Anglo-Saxon settlement, 'Niweshum', meaning the new houses; but all trace of the settlement has long gone. It became a manor, then an estate, and was bought by the Corporation in 1846 with the idea of opening the first public park in Liverpool. But money was short, and only in 1868 was work begun and Newsham House converted to become the lodging house for judges attending the Liverpool Assizes. The house accommodated Queen Victoria on her visit to the new city in 1886, and is still used for VIP visits today. From the windows of Newsham House the spire of St Oswald's church in Old Swan can be seen over the trees of Newsham Park, as well as the large Park Hospital and Seamen's Orphanage. This was built by Alfred Waterhouse, the renowned Liverpool architect, and although rather grim to modern eyes it is certainly a landmark building. More attractive is the church of St John the Baptist

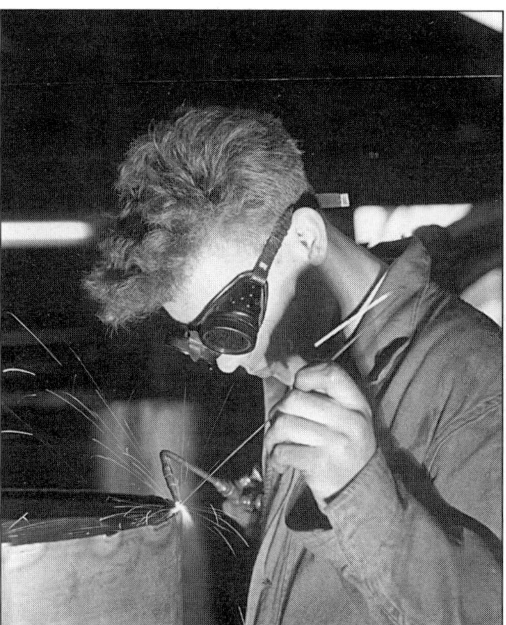

Apprentices in the City Engineer's depot, Breckside Park, May 1961.

on the corner of Green Lane, built in the late 1860s by George Frederick Bodley. He was one of the giants of the Victorian Gothic Revival, and built a very beautiful church in Tuebrook which Quentin Hughes described as 'one of the most impressive of the suburban churches' in Liverpool. Almost opposite is the pretty modern church of St Cecilia, and nearby the closed Jewish cemetery, one of a handful across the city.

The imposing Seamen's Orphanage, later the Park Hospital. It was designed by Alfred Waterhouse and built between 1871 and 1874.

Stoneycroft

The landmark Stanley Abattoir in June 1959.

'Stoneycroft is the more imposing name for the suburb of Old Swan,' wrote Liverpool historian Michael O'Mahony in 1930. The district sits snugly between Green Lane, Queens Drive, West Derby Road and Prescot Road, one of the neatest of Liverpool's suburbs. For many centuries it was an agricultural district along the banks of the Tew Brook, but from the mid-1800s it was developed by Richard Radcliffe. Radcliffe was a lawyer with good connections, and laid out Stoneycroft on a plan derived from Bloomsbury in London, with wide streets, squares, mixed housing, gardens, and lavish tree planting. In effect he built a model estate, an early garden suburb. The trees came from Croxteth Park, where Radcliffe had family connections, and were planted 'for the purpose of beautifying the new garden suburb.' He also laid out the attractive Derwent Square, which was described by James Hoult as 'aristocratic' because of the number of judges, army officers, clergymen, lawyers and businessmen who lived there before World War Two.

Stoneycroft really only dates from Radcliffe's plans, but he was helped by the area becoming prosperous in the 1830s with the arrival of the railway and the cattle

market. In 1831 St Anne's church was built, in an area composed of small farms and larger houses and still very rural; the replacement church built 50 years later still stands in a large and pleasant churchyard on Prescot Road. The following year a cattle market was established on Prescot Road, which was replaced by the great Stanley Abattoir in the early 1930s.

Radcliffe's energy and money ran out in 1867, and his plans were abandoned, but following his ideas others built in the same vein in the same area. Shaftesbury

Terrace, between Brooklands Road and Prescot Road, was built in 1871 as model workmen's dwellings, an attempt to build decent housing for the working classes. Gradually the model estate was surrounded and absorbed by the developments of Tuebrook and Old Swan, but today Derwent Square and the elegant houses of Derwent Road form a small conservation area, although too many of the houses are currently in poor condition or even boarded up.

Knotty Ash

Knotty Ash is one of the few districts of Liverpool known beyond the city's boundaries. It is famous because of the absurd humour of Ken Dodd, who invented jam butty mines, snuff quarries and a broken biscuit repair works for his imaginary fiefdom. Although Knotty Ash is his home, he apparently used the place name because audiences didn't believe that it was a real place.

Knotty Ash was originally part of the huge township of West Derby and is supposed to have gained its name from an old ash tree, which stood on the site of the Knotty Ash Hotel at the top of Thomas Lane. Yates and Perry's map of 1768 seems to have been the first mention of Knotty Ash as an independent area. Like Old Swan, Knotty Ash grew in importance because of the coach roads; there was a toll bar here, and a space used by entertainers. The first mail coach to Prescot from Liverpool ran through the district in 1767, and the coaches to Manchester also ran through Knotty Ash. There were also horse buses, which ran between Liverpool and the Turk's Head Inn at Knotty Ash, and at one time this service was run by the grandfather of James Hoult, the Liverpool antiquarian and writer. The Turk's Head was built on East Prescot Road in the 17th century and demolished as recently as 1959.

The shopping centre for the Dovecot estate, proud and clean and nearly new when photographed in July 1933.

PUBLIC LIBRARY
BRIDE & BIRTHDAY
CUBBON BROS
CAKE MAKERS
PEGRAMS STORES

Knotty Ash was a very small village at the centre of a district that had both farmland and big estates. The district was built up in the 20th century with houses for the people of Liverpool. As in Everton, the names of the lost mansions still resound through local street names and housing developments today. Finch House stood on Finch Lane between the late 1770s and 1912, and was built by Richard Gildart, who had been a local MP some 40 years previously. Dovecot was an 18th-century house with a mediaeval pedigree, and stood in the middle of Dovecot Park. One of the big houses was Ashfield, built by James Clemens, who was originally from the Isle of Man. He owned a great deal of property in the Knotty

Ash/Broadgreen area, and in 1775–6 he was mayor of Liverpool. In that year he erected a pillar on the corner of Thomas Lane and Thingwall Lane to direct travellers to Broadgreen and Knotty Ash, and had his own initials and the date carved into it as well. Clemens was a builder, and it was once said that a peculiar local style of Gothic window marked his buildings. His house Ashfield stood on the other side of Thingwall Lane from his pillar, but has since been demolished.

The most interesting buildings in Knotty Ash are on or around Thomas Lane, which runs from East Prescot Road to Rocky Lane at the M62. The Lane is busy for most of its length with traffic between the motorway and the huge Broadgreen Hospital, but has some sturdy Victorian mansions. At the top of a quieter stretch of Thomas Lane stands the church of St John the Evangelist, built between 1835 and 1837 in a defensive and uncertain Gothic manner. Between the church and East Prescot Road are a number of interesting buildings, and Thomas Lane culminates in Little Bongs, a row of 18th-century cottages hidden off East Prescot Road.

The distinctive façade of the Calvary Baptist church visible across a speeding East Prescot Road in December 1958.

Thingwall

Thingwall is one of Liverpool's truly lost villages. It lies between Knotty Ash and Bowring Park, but no longer has any particular landmarks. The name is Norse, and means 'Parliament Field', and Derek Whale suggests that Thingwall was a place of council for the Scandinavians who settled in this area in the centuries after the Romans left. The manor of Thingwall was given by King John in exchange for Smithdown manor, in order for him to extend his hunting park at Toxteth, but apart from a number of local roads there is no longer anything to suggest that there was ever a settlement or village centre here at all. The only building of note is Thingwall Hall, built in the late 18th century and now owned by the Brothers of Charity who run it as a rest home.

Further reading

James Hoult, *A Short Story of Stoneycroft*, Liverpool, 1939.

Quentin Hughes, *Liverpool City of Architecture*, Liverpool, 1999.

Michael O'Mahony, *Liverpool Districts*, Liverpool Echo articles, 1930s.

Richard Radcliffe Stanley, *Notes on Stanley and Neighbourhood*, Old Swan, 1910.

Derek Whale, *Lost Villages of Liverpool* Parts I and II, 1985.

QUEENS DRIVE

Queens Drive is not a district or suburb of Liverpool, but this great inner ring road connects many of the huge north-eastern suburbs of the city with the city centre, and indeed enabled them to be built. It represents an expansion of the modern city unimaginable to the merchants of the 18th and 19th century, and for a time was an outer limit, an invisible city wall, for Liverpool. Yet in speeding up and improving road links with the city centre, it enabled great new suburbs to be built, and today it is many miles from open countryside.

The success of Queens Drive was due to the energy and foresight of two men, John Alexander Brodie and Lancelot Keay. Brodie was the City Engineer responsible for the imaginative Otterspool Promenade, an idea that the city authorities

The construction of Queens Drive at Wavertree in February 1909.

Queens Drive at Walton. This was the first stretch to be built, so it is finished if not developed in this view looking towards Larkhill in 1909.

The Fiveways, Childwall, September 1911. This stretch of Queens Drive was finished but not yet built up.

have since extended right into the city centre. He also designed the football goal net. Lancelot Keay was Director of Housing for the Corporation between 1925 and 1938, and took on the additional responsibility of City Architect between 1938 and 1948. He had an immense impact on the city landscape, and built over 30,000 apartments and houses to solve the city's chronic housing problems. Quentin Hughes feels that together the two men did 'brilliant work in fashioning the outskirts of the city.'

The notion of a road ringing the city had been discussed since the early 1800s, and especially since the mid-century when the city was starting to spill out past the 18th-century boundaries in earnest. Brodie was especially interested in the 'circular boulevard' plan of 1853 which would have provided parks for the working classes and, in its own words, would have been 'a great convenience to the public in general'. But although there had been piecemeal attempts to link the city along its circumference before, it was Brodie's vision and enterprise that finally began the building of a road around the city. Originally three concentric rings were imagined, but only the middle road, Queens Drive, was ever built.

The first section was begun at Rice Lane, because it was one of the original radial roads from the city centre, and the main route to Preston and the north. Work began on the Cherry Lane section in 1904, with the extension from Walton to Larkhill being built in 1909. In building the huge road around the city, Brodie adapted many existing roads and lanes. Some were widened and straightened to fit the plan, and other gaps were filled with new roads. By 1910 there was road-building from Broadgreen Road to Childwall Road, and a stretch from Allerton Road to the London & North Western Railway at Mossley Hill. Photographs of Queens Drive at this time have a haunted, misty quality to them; the road looks raw, unfinished, and above all empty. It resembles World War One transport roads crossing strange fields, no longer rural but not yet urban.

'It is proposed eventually,' wrote Brodie in 1911, 'to continue the boulevard across the London & North Western, skirting Sefton Park, to join Aigburth Road, the main highway running south to Garston.' The boulevard was burrowing underneath the railway by 1915, but the link with Aigburth Road is vague and ill defined; Queens Drive stops gently at the road around Sefton Park, at a roundabout under tall trees on the quietest stretch of the road, and the grand junction with Aigburth Road was never built.

The creation of Queens Drive was a massive undertaking. John Brodie's circumferential boulevard connected Bootle and Walton with Sefton Park, in a great

Queens Drive
from Menlove
Avenue on a sunny
day in 1911.

crescent around the city. It was a road on the classical model, with roundabouts and junctions connecting Queens Drive with the radial roads into the city, like the spokes of a wheel connecting hub with rim. Existing radial routes such as Prescot Road and Aigburth Road were widened, and new routes into the city were created. Edge Lane Drive, Walton Hall Avenue and Menlove Avenue were laid out to improve access to and from Queens Drive. On Walton Hall Avenue Brodie's engineers reverently went around the small mound and clump of trees that was all that survived of Walton Hall, and on Menlove Avenue costs were partially defrayed by agreements with the tramway authorities who laid track down the central reservation.

Queens Drive opened up enormous areas of the city's hinterland to new building, and it is arguable that the new road only really came into its own in the 1920s and 1930s when Liverpool needed a huge amount of new homes to ease overcrowding and to house people being cleared from city-centre slums. The municipal authorities acquired the crumbling or derelict country estates of Lark Hill and Norris Green, and alongside Brodie's 'circumferential boulevard' Lancelot Keay laid out elegant housing schemes. 'The houses are neo-Georgian in style,' wrote Quentin Hughes in 1964, 'carefully detailed and well proportioned, with considerable subtlety. They are placed in areas of grass and trees and are amongst the best examples of municipal housing undertaken at the time.' Lancelot Keay designed property all over the city, but Quentin Hughes feels that his best suburban work is to be seen along Queens Drive, at Knotty Ash and Norris Green. Lancelot Keay's work in Liverpool deserves a book to itself, but it is some measure of his success that five of the 'garden estates' he laid out across the city were declared conservation areas in 1971.

Queens Drive still connects many of the main routes into and out of Liverpool, and is the defining symbol of its outlying districts, linking huge swathes of suburbia with the city centre. With the vast increase in road traffic from the middle of the 20th century onwards, Queens Drive truly came into its own, and today only the tree-lined stretch at Mossley Hill is relatively quiet; its success meant that in the late 1960s the road was turned into a dual carriageway and flyovers were built at the Rocket and Rice Lane to improve the flow of traffic.

Queens Drive is a microcosm of Liverpool suburbia. It passes through semi-detached Allerton and Childwall as well as council estates of Lancelot Keay's 'subtle and well-mannered' architecture. It connects Bootle with Aigburth and enables

New houses at Clubmoor in 1920.

Queens Drive under construction in the early 20th century. The Drive opened up huge areas for Liverpool's expansion.

traffic to reach almost any part of the city without travelling into the city centre. It is a superb achievement, and its success and continued popularity amply justify the city's faith in Brodie's vision.

Further reading

John Brodie, *The Development of Liverpool and its Circumferential Boulevard,* Town Planning Review, 1910.

Quentin Hughes, *Liverpool City of Architecture,* Liverpool, 1999.

Quentin Hughes, *Seaport,* Liverpool, 1964.

Liverpool Heritage Bureau, *Liverpool Conservation Areas,* 1979.

SPEKE, HUNTS CROSS AND HALEWOOD

Speke was laid out between the 1930s and 1950s as a self-contained township, with links to the city and work available in the industrial estate developed at the same time. New housing was needed to cut the council's waiting lists of over 30,000 people, to aid its slum clearance programme and to ease overcrowding. The new township was planned and designed by Sir Lancelot Keay, the city's Director of Housing and also City Architect for many years between the wars. Speke must have seemed like the future of Liverpool; it had wide boulevards and bright factories, good houses with gardens, even garages for the anticipated rise in car ownership. Crowning it all was the city's brand new Art Deco airport. The estate was praised by Peter Fleetwood-Hesketh as being 'beautifully laid out' with the houses being 'of admirable design and of a kind that gives new hope for the future of small-scale domestic architecture'; the development was 'one of the most ambitious municipal projects of its kind'. The new township was begun in 1936 and finished in the late

Speke industrial estate, 1939.

Edward's Lane, Speke industrial estate, in September 1946. A quiet afternoon apart from the figure lurching unsteadily across a roof to the right of the picture.

1950s, after a break of some years during World War Two. It is laid out on a formal, classical plan dictated by the flat landscape, the absence of natural features, and the regularity of the boundaries. As Quentin Hughes has remarked, in his book *Liverpool City of Architecture,* perhaps the design lacks height, but mature trees and church spires compensate for this.

Under the fabric of modern Speke the farming landscape it displaced still asserts itself. Speke ends abruptly; there is no melting into the countryside, no hinterland of half-town half-country. One side of the road is township, the other is field. Haywains still pass through Speke from the fields near Hale, there are skylarks and house martins in the air above the airfield, and above all many road names reflect the farmland they were built upon; Goldfinch Farm Road, Blackhall Farm Road, Little Heath Road, all remember the rural landscape transformed by Keay's builders. Some road names survived the upheaval, albeit in a very different form; Speke Town Lane and Woodend Lane can be found on maps of the area from before the 1930s, and the latter in particular is an ancient road, which has links with modern Woodend Avenue in Halewood. Most interesting is Conleach Road, in the very centre of modern Speke. 'At the boundary of Speke, Halewood and Hale there is a piece of land called Conleach,' said the *Victoria History* in 1907. 'Here formal challenge fights used to take place between the inhabitants of the adjoining villages.' The churchyard around the Victorian sandstone church of All Saints has the graves of the farmers who lived here before the development of the 1930s, and their solid names are carved on numerous graves and the memorial from World War One: Raper, Dunbavin, Leadbetter, Sumner, Wyke and Whyke, Barber. There were Byrons living in the large farm of Sutton Grange, swallowed in the 1930s by the old airfield, and Mawdsleys in Woodend Farm.

These farmers might well have been tenants of Speke Hall, the oldest building by far in the district. The Hall was built over many years from the 13th century near to 'the Clough', a stream which on its way to the river provided water for a defensive moat, and which is still marked on maps today. Speke Hall is now owned and run by the National Trust and the City Council as one of Liverpool's top tourist attractions. The lands administered for centuries from the Hall were described at the end of the 19th century as 'some of the best wheat growing land in the Hundred (of West Derby)…

Post-war optimism; the airport bus at Speke in 1962.

An aerial picture of Speke in January 1939, with the lines of new roads superimposed by the City Engineers. The township can be seen in the far right of the picture.

there are scattered plantations amongst open fields, where barley and oats as well as wheat grow well…' and it is possible that the name Speke derives from the Anglo-Saxon 'spic' meaning bacon, and indicating pasture for pigs, possibly of oak woods. For centuries the district was farmland, dotted with small clusters of farm-hamlets, with the shore to the river dotted with the fishing hamlets of Oglet, Dungeon Point and Hale.

The 1960s and 1970s saw a low point in Speke's history. When it was planned and laid out the township was too dependent for employment on the industrial estate, and when factories closed and companies moved away, unemployment rose. Speke developed an unenviable reputation for decay and poverty, with their associated problems of crime and drug abuse. Even the airport became something of a joke, as only freight companies seemed to use it and it suffered by comparison with Manchester's gleaming terminal 40 miles away.

But in recent years Speke has been

regenerated. Great improvements have been made to the housing stock and the industrial estate, which now form a neat and impressive gateway to the city. The old airfield site has been transformed into a smart industrial park, with new uses being found for the old hangars, and the Art Deco airport buildings have been renovated, extended, and converted into a smart, award-winning hotel. The new airport is the first in the country to be named after an individual, and the Liverpool John Lennon Airport has been well placed to take advantage of the trend in 'budget travel'; a number of small airlines and holiday companies use the facilities at Speke in preference to bigger, more expensive, airports. Much of modern residential Speke is well maintained housing with large gardens, wide roads and mature trees, and, although the district has had problems with vandalism and neglect, it is a considerable improvement on the suburban decay of only a decade ago.

Hunts Cross

The Cross possibly marked the route from Speke to Childwall church, or the boundary of the three parishes of Speke, Much Woolton and Halewood. It first appears on a map of 1848, but the remains lay derelict for many years until they were re-erected in the early 20th century by Alderman Mather, who was also responsible for restoring Woolton Cross. For many years a farming district, Hunts Cross today is an area given over almost entirely to 20th century housing, between

Macketts Lane before resurfacing work, November 1954.

the industrial estate of Speke and the wooded heights of Woolton. 'A distinct and separate community of business and factory executives, workers and residents, living and working together,' wrote the local historian Eric McKie in 1946, and although patterns of work have changed since the 1940s, Hunts Cross is still largely a quiet residential district today.

Halewood

Halewood is an ancient district, the name of which reflects its origins as the woodland of Hale manor. Derek Whale records the fact that King John had a hunting ground here in the early 1200s, but the woods had been largely cleared by the early 16th century and for much of its history Halewood has been an agricultural district. Even today there is a clear boundary between housing and field; this is the very edge of the city. Halewood was described at the end of the 19th century as '...bare and flat with wide open fields, principally cultivated, yielding crops of barley, oats, wheat and root crops such as turnips and mangel wurzels.' A hundred and eighty years earlier wheat, barley, oats, hay, peas, beans, vetches and potatoes were grown in Halewood.

The only building of any age in Halewood was the Old Hutte, a mansion built by the Ireland family in the 13th century, at about the same time as Speke Hall. But

The walls of the Olde Hutte in June 1961, numbered for reassembly before being dismantled.

the two houses had very different histories and by the early 20th century most of the Old Hutte had been destroyed apart from a massive gate-house, which had been turned into a farmhouse. Enough survived to become a rural museum or store for the Liverpool Museums, but with the discovery of extensive dry rot the plan was abandoned and the building was demolished in the early 1950s. There is still an Old Hutte Lane in Halewood, but the ruins have long since disapp-eared under the massive industrial development of the old Ford car plant. The second half of the 20th century saw great tracts of housing being built in Halewood, and the old district was built over from the 1930s to the 1960s as the huge factories between here and Speke provided work. Today Halewood and Hunts Cross are indistinguishable from the suburban sprawl at the edge of the city, but some parts have kept their links with the countryside, at the very edge of Liverpool.

Further reading

Ronald Bradbury, *Liverpool Builds 1945–1965*, City of Liverpool Public Records Office, 1965.

Peter Fleetwood-Hesketh, *Murray's Guide to Lancashire*, 1955.

Eric McKie, *Handbook of Hunts Cross*, 1949.

Victoria History of Lancashire Volume III, 1907.

Derek Whale, *Lost Villages of Liverpool* Part II, 1985.

The Face of Speke 1084–1952, private research project, 1952.

TOXTETH

Toxteth is a relatively small part of Liverpool 8, the postal district that sprawls from Sefton Park to the University and along Park Road and Mill Lane to meet the city proper at Upper Parliament Street. Yet the two names are interchangeable in the popular imagination, especially since the riots of 1981, so 'Toxteth' is used here to describe the whole district. It is an inner-city suburb, almost not 'sub-urban' at all; the inner city has grown as the city has expanded. Today it is part of the awkward mythology of Liverpool, but Toxteth has a long and interesting history stretching back to the Anglo-Saxon Dark Ages, to King John, and to the English Civil War. Toxteth has links with early astronomy, with the early years of two of America's greatest universities, and has been home to the city's artists and musicians since the 1940s.

A Stone Age axe-head was found in Toxteth Park, and the district is mentioned in the Domesday Book as 'Stochestede', an Anglo-Saxon name implying a stockaded area to protect livestock. But Toxteth's history begins in modern terms in 1207, when King John established the borough of 'Leverpul' as a port for Ireland. Alongside the creation of a new town and port, he established a royal hunting park by buying the manor of Toxteth from the Molyneux family, giving a manor in Litherland in exchange. The Molyneux kept a close eye on their property, however; they were Chief

Foresters in the reign of Henry VI and regained the property when it was deforested in 1604.

Toxteth Park stretched from St James's Church to Aigburth Vale and from Smithdown Road to the river, and was entirely reserved for the use of the royal family. The Crown employed a Master Huntsman and 49 men to police the park, as well as 10 horses, two packs of dogs, and 52 spaniels. There were two lodges to mark the Park's entrances and provide accommodation for these officials. One stood on the site of Otterspool Station, and is covered in the chapter on Aigburth.

An aerial view of Toxteth in 1903. St Gabriel's church spire on Beaufort Street can be seen to the left of the picture, with the stump of the windmill on Mill Lane visible to the right.

Roadworks on Princes Avenue/Granby Street in 1905, when local houses employed maids.

The other stood on the corner of Ullet Road and Lodge Lane (perhaps once known as the lane to the lodge) and the private house there today, Park Lodge, has elements of the 13th-century lodge within it. King John also bought the neighbouring manor of Smithdown (named as Esmedune in the Domesday Book) to extend the park, and gave the manor of Thingwall in exchange. Although there is no evidence that John or his descendants ever came here to hunt, Toxteth Park was left as a reserve for the beasts of the chase for 400 years.

The Crown sold Toxteth Park at the beginning of the 17th century, and Puritan families were enticed from the Midlands by the Catholic Lord Molyneux with lands along the river that ran down Park Road to the Dingle. They are remembered today in the street names of the 'Holy Land', Moses, Isaac and David Streets, off Park Road, and it was these Puritans who built the Ancient Chapel of Toxteth from 1618 onwards. The early modern cultural life of Toxteth revolved around the Ancient Chapel. It was nominally attached to the Church of England but was never consecrated, and from its earliest days it attracted radical thinkers and preachers. At

the turn of the 17th century, Richard Mather arrived in the district as a schoolmaster, although he was only 15 years old himself. He responded vigorously to the district's Puritanism, and became increasingly radical in his thinking; so much so that he attracted the attention of the Established church authorities. 'Tradition has handed down the memory of nocturnal assemblages in the valley of the Dingle,' wrote James Picton, 'where the Puritans met by stealth to listen to the exhortations of their beloved Pastor,' but soon even these desperate measures proved inadequate. Richard Mather was 'harassed and persecuted' and in 1635 sailed for America. His ministry in the New World was a great success, and the link between churches in Toxteth and New England is still maintained. Richard's son Increase Mather was President of Harvard, and his grandson Cotton Mather (supposedly piqued at not being asked to follow his father) was instrumental in founding the University of Yale. These two academics were closely involved in the notorious Salem witch trials.

The Ancient Chapel continued to be a centre for local religious nonconformity, and it has long been rumoured that Cromwell's soldiers camped around it during

An elegant Hartington Road in 1905.

Voelas Street, off High Park Street, in July 1911.

Next page: There was vicious poverty in Toxteth. These court dwellings stood off Back Chester Street in November 1911.

the English Civil War of the 1640s. The Chapel also nurtured Jeremiah Horrocks, born in 1619 in the old park lodge in modern Otterspool Park. In 1639 he was the first astronomer to predict and observe the transit of Venus across the sun, and Derek Whale comments that but for his early death at the age of 23, he 'would have joined the ranks of men like Galileo'. Commemorative tablets in the Ancient Chapel and the iron church of St Michael are all the recognition his hometown has given him.

The industrious Puritans of the Ancient Chapel rapidly turned the old hunting park into farmland, and Toxteth was agricultural until the end of the 18th century. Yates and Perry's map from 1768 has many identifiable roads running across a landscape of fields and meadows, and the 1769 map of the last Earl of Sefton has the fields named after their owners or their nature; Little Sea Hey near the river, Birch Meadow, and Chapel Hey behind the Ancient Chapel. In 1771 a 52-acre farm

on the boundary of Liverpool was laid out for streets by the Earl of Sefton, who obtained an Act of Parliament in 1775 to grant building leases. The new town was to be called New Liverpool, but eventually Harrington was settled on 'in compliment to Isabella, first Countess of Sefton, daughter of the second Earl of Harrington.' Only the 'parish church' of this new town survives; St James's on Parliament Street, built in 1775 by Cuthbert Bisbrowne, who took 'the most active part' in carrying out the scheme for the new town.

The first part of the Park to be built up was the land west of Mill Street, between Northumberland Street and Parliament Street, whose name commemorates the Act that enabled modern Toxteth to develop. Yet Picton comments that the development was slow; Harrington was not a success, and it was the resourceful and determined Victorians who turned Toxteth from a rural district into a suburb of their new city. The land was too close to the thriving docks and the city to remain rural for long, although some of the old farm lanes were simply modernised to link parts of the district as they had for hundreds of years; Ullet Road, Croxteth Road, Lodge Lane. Ullet Road shows its age by being a Saxon word for a little owl, and there are still owls on the road today. Development kept pace with the building of the south docks and later industries (such as the Herculaneum Pottery and the huge Mersey Forge) on the river.

An imposing town hall and civic buildings were built in the district's highest point, on High Park Street, and a great reservoir built. The Victorian wealthy built elegant Italianate houses along Princes Avenue and around the new greenery of Prince's Park, which was designed by Joseph Paxton and laid out in the early 1840s

by local landowner Richard Vaughan Yates. Quentin Hughes argues that Princes Park was the beginning of the transformation of south Liverpool into residential areas for the expanding city, although at first it was not a public park. The gates were locked at night and only the people whose houses backed onto the park had access for evening walks, but then it was partially the money raised from selling the house plots that had enabled the park to be built. It is possible that Decimus Burton was involved in some of the finer detail of the park, such as the cast-iron gates onto Princes Avenue and the lost gatehouse at the same entrance. Burton is unfairly obscure today, but he laid out Hyde Park in 1825, and was employed designing the new town of Fleetwood at the time that Princes Park was being laid out. It has been suggested that Decimus Burton also designed some of the houses around the park, and it is even possible that he designed property on Peel Street. He worked in the Dingle for Richard Vaughan Yates's brother. (This house was later the home of Matthew Arnold's sister. It was leaving here in 1888 that the poet and social reformer suffered a heart attack and collapsed, dying on Park Road opposite the Ancient Chapel, which is why the local primary school still carries his name.)

The rooftops of Grafton and Upper Mann Streets in 1934. The steep roofs of the Southern Hospital on Caryl Street can be seen to the left, with the misty chimney of the Mersey Brewery on the right.

In addition to their elegant houses, the Victorians gave the district one of the most attractive cemeteries in Liverpool. Toxteth Cemetery was laid out in 1853, the same year as the huge necropolis in Anfield, but being built on a gentle slope has a softer, less utilitarian feel to it. Toxteth is a romantic cemetery, the more so for being so visible and immediate, easily accessible from busy Smithdown Road. The graves mostly contain the high Victorian worthies who lived in the district at the end of the 19th century, and the grandest tombs cluster around the central axis of the cemetery like gigantic chess pieces, adding a note of Alice in Wonderland surreality to the place. The winding paths lead under melancholy chestnut trees, which are now mature enough to give the cemetery a frisson of Victorian gloom. Until a few years ago, the tower of Sefton Hospital next door loomed over the cemetery, but the hospital has largely gone and an enormous supermarket is there today.

The merchants and sea captains of Toxteth however, are only half the picture. In laying out the new town of Harrington 'a grave error was committed,' wrote James Picton, 'the results of which have been very serious and will operate injuriously for ages to come'. Between the grand roads there spread 'mean, narrow streets, filled with close gloomy courts into which as many dwellings as possible were packed, irrespective of light and air.' Much of the property built for the next 80 or 90 years between Park Road and the docks was of an appallingly low standard. In 1835 semi-rural Toxteth became part of Liverpool, but this did not prevent the remaining countryside being bricked over by slums. The later Victorians began the process of clearing this property, but the last were not cleared until the 1930s, when the large housing blocks of Warwick Gardens and Caryl Gardens were built by the gifted team assembled by City Architect and Housing Director Lancelot Keay. They must have seemed clean and healthy to the people rehoused from the crumbling slums, but they too have been demolished, as housing needs have changed. Across the city the municipal authority now houses people in bungalows or two-storey semi-detached houses, with gardens and a small driveway.

Toxteth is now known far beyond the borders of Liverpool, and was for a time a by-word for inner city decay and even urban revolution. In the summer of 1981 a series of localised disturbances known as the Toxteth Riots caught the attention of the world's media, and the famous images of barricades and burning cars were paraded on television. The riots were never as widespread as the media pretended, but a number of similar events in other deprived inner cities caused the national government to devise a policy of nationwide urban regeneration, which has continued ever since. The riots led directly to the creation of the Merseyside

A superb photograph of J. Bore's North Hill Street works in December 1954, with a group of curious workers visible in the courtyard.

New flats and half-demolished buildings – Mill Street and Park Street in May 1960.

Rich funerary carving in Toxteth cemetery.

Development Corporation and the International Garden Festival in Otterspool in 1984, and Toxteth is now slowly benefiting from the public and private money being used to develop Britain's inner cities. The municipal authority is building semi-detached houses with small gardens and driveways to replace the undesirable red-brick Victorian terracing, and the private sector is redeveloping the large apartment houses that overlook them into luxury flats. Rich and poor still live alongside each other.

Yet Liverpool dislikes and mistrusts Toxteth, and sees it through more mythology than any other district. Toxteth is certainly like no other district of Liverpool; sandwiched between the docks, Chinatown, and the University, it has an edge, a creativity, a cosmopolitanism, that marks it out from the rest of the city. The district around Falkner Square and Catherine Street is Liverpool's red-light district, but also her bohemia, with artists and musicians living in flats and squats. Granby Street, currently being massively redeveloped, has long been the centre of Liverpool's Afro-Caribbean community, some of whom can trace their ancestry back to 18th-century slaves. Black sailors from overseas established clubs for fellow expatriates on Parliament Street and Princes Avenue, which became places to dance and hear new and interesting music in the late 1950s, the origin of Liverpool's rhythm and blues explosion of the 1960s. Toxteth is mostly home to ordinary working-class people, black and white, and this community produced Ringo Starr and Billy Fury, among others, but no matter; students live in Toxteth, as do poets and musicians, madmen and writers, painters and dancers, and Liverpool is a conservative city which looks on such people with distaste and unease.

Walking the streets of Toxteth today is a varied and interesting experience. Some of the district, particularly the streets nearest the city, has been

gentrified and developed, and the old Georgian houses have been restored to their past splendour. Falkner Square, Catherine Street and the wide roads of Huskisson and Canning Streets on the very edge of the city have seen property prices rise dramatically in the past few years, leading Liverpool novelist Linda Grant to call this area 'Liverpool's Islington,' referring to the influx of money into an old area convenient for the city; but 'Liverpool's Spitalfields' might be nearer the mark, with its rich mixture of races and cultures, its bohemianism, its history. But some areas of Toxteth are untouched by this redevelopment, and are as poor and deprived as anywhere in the city; once again, in this unique suburb, rich and poor live cheek by jowl.

Further reading

Robert Griffiths, *The History of the Royal and Ancient Park of Toxteth*, reprinted 2000.

James Picton, *Memorials of Liverpool* Volume II, Liverpool, 1873.

Scouse Press Maps of Liverpool 2; A Map of Toxteth Park, 1769.

George Yates and William Perry 'Map of Leverpool and Environs', 1768.

VAUXHALL

Athol Street in November 1957, photographed shortly before clearance.

Vauxhall is a recent addition to the suburbs of Liverpool, a consequence of the town's increasing industrialisation at the end of the 18th century. For many years the area between Everton and the docks was farmland, crossed by lanes connecting Liverpool to Bevington Bush and Kirkdale and the small fishing communities on the shoreline. Modern Vauxhall grew up around these old roads – Vauxhall Road was for many years called Pinfold Lane, Mile House Lane became Great Howard Street, and there is still a fragment of Love Lane, once an 18th-century farm track and now a quiet industrial street, next to the railway viaduct. It was an attractive district, and popular with walkers as it was so close to the small port.

The district was largely rural until the end of the 18th century and the construction of the Leeds–Liverpool Canal, which cut through the fields to a basin in Leeds Street. Bridges were thrown across the canal and streets of workshops and warehouses built on the fields nearest the town. The sedate promenade at Maiden's Green disappeared under Leeds Street, and the Georgian pleasure gardens further out at Gildart's Gardens and Summer Seat were built up with courts of sub-standard housing.

Number 11 Court, Burlington Street, typical of the cramped slums that once infested Vauxhall.

The workshops and factories connected with the docks, the railway and the Leeds–Liverpool canal transformed the area, and Vauxhall grew from farmland into an industrial area with an appalling reputation for squalid housing and overcrowding. In the 1840s and 1850s the area became home to large numbers of Irish immigrants, driven from their homes in Ireland by the consequences of the

Great Famine, and the origin of the great Irish Catholic communities of Scotland Road. Clarence Dock now has a plaque commemorating its history as the main place of entry for the huge numbers of displaced Irish who poured into Liverpool at this time – up to 1.3 million in as few as five or six years. Many of them settled in Vauxhall, as there was work on the docks and the canal. The largely Catholic Irish brought their politics with them, and Irish Nationalism was locally very strong – during the early years of agitation for Home Rule, Vauxhall was a hotbed of Fenianism, and a cache of weapons was once found in the cellars of the Summer Seat public house.

From the mid-20th century, however, Vauxhall declined. The docks were badly bombed during World War Two, and work dried up as industry began to drift away. In the 1960s and 1970s much of the poor-quality housing was demolished and the inhabitants rehoused, often not too far from where they used to live. The residents of the Eldon Street district, in particular, chose not to be moved away from the area. Proud of their descent from the Irish immigrants of 150 years ago, they formed themselves into 'the Eldonians'. They worked with housing associations and architects to build the Eldonian Village, a neat landscape of semi-detached houses

A view of the rooftops and narrow alleyways of Hopwood and Benledi Streets, 1934.

Houses and industrial buildings in the Athol Street area during redevelopment in November 1957.

The old Burlington Street bridge over the Leeds–Liverpool Canal in 1903. This fine classical structure was replaced by a more sturdy bridge in 1905.

Very poor housing in Eldon Street in 1910.

The prefabricated tenement block designed by John Brodie for Eldon Street in 1903, photographed a couple of years later.

A different view of the tenement block on the same day, 11 May 1906, showing premises on Vauxhall Road.

and large gardens alongside the canal. New plans are currently being aired for the regeneration of the canal and its possible extension to the city's waterfront and even the Albert Dock, and if Vauxhall is revitalised by this it will be in no small part due to the commitment and hard work of the Eldonians.

The 'grass-roots' regeneration work of the Eldonians has done much to stabilise the area, and today Vauxhall is home to small businesses and quiet streets of good-quality modern houses. The huge industrial buildings and streets of terraces have largely gone, although there are still reminders of its industrial past to be found; there are solid iron bridges over the canal, rusting cranes, and wharves overgrown with wildflowers.

Further reading

Frank O'Connor, *Liverpool Our City Our Heritage*, Liverpool, 1995.

James Picton, *Memorials of Liverpool* Volume II, Liverpool, 1873.

Old Vauxhall – A Miscellany of Local History, researched and compiled by the Vauxhall Community Archives Project, 1994.

WALTON AND FAZAKERLEY

Walton is probably the oldest village making up modern suburban Liverpool. It was already at least six or eight hundred years old at the time of the Domesday survey in the late 11th century, and it is so old that the origins of its name have been lost. Walton is a common English place name, and writers have given Liverpool's Walton a variety of explanations. Most agree that 'ton' derives from the Anglo-Saxon word for a settlement, but the 'wal' causes difficulties. Some have argued that it refers to the large number of wells in the area, others that it means a wood, so Walton would mean a settlement in a wood; the area was thickly forested at least until the 13th century. Still other writers have suggested 'walled town', but 'wal' could also refer to the ancient Britons that the Saxons found as they invaded Britain, and gave Wales and the Welsh their names. Walton could therefore mean 'town of the Britons', referring to a settlement that lasted longer than surrounding villages

Walton Park gates in 1924, with curious onlookers.

Rice Lane and Walton Library on a day without too much traffic in 1929.

against the Saxons, or became a haven for refugees from other villages. A stone circle has even been suggested for Walton Hill, destroyed by monks from Lindisfarne bringing Christianity to the area in the later Dark Ages. This is given some credence by Peter Howell Williams's comment 'the circular shape of Liverpool's original parish churchyard is alleged to denote that the Druids once used this ground as a place of worship.' The small street behind Walton church is still called Walton Village, but has no buildings older than the 19th century; old Walton survives today in the embattled 17th-century schoolhouse, one of only a handful of old school buildings in the city, and the church of St Mary.

St Mary's church at Walton is on a very old Christian site. It is possible that the first church was built in the 10th century, and was built of wood or wattle and daub. Liverpudlians walked to the important church at Walton for centuries, and only in 1699 with the town expanding was Liverpool granted parish status. (In a final act of gentle homage, many of the gravestones from the cleared St Peter's churchyard in the city centre were removed to Walton Park Cemetery in 1922.) Walton parish at one time included Formby, and the royal park Simonswood near

A spectacular display on Elm Road for the Coronation in 1953.

The junction of County Road, Queens Drive and Rice Lane in early 1952. The huge flyover now covers this site.

*Old Walton –
Church flags and
the tower of St
Mary's church,
October 1952.*

Kirkby, as well as Kirkby itself, Fazakerley, Bootle, Kirkdale, Everton, West Derby, Liverpool, and Toxteth Park, another royal estate. The first stone church was erected in 1361, but the existing building is no older than the 19th century, having been rebuilt and restored over the centuries. An ancient wooden cross shaft was discovered in 1946 under the floor of the nave as the church was being restored after bomb damage in World War Two. The eminent Liverpool sculptor Edward Carter-Preston, who also designed sculpture for the Anglican Cathedral, was closely involved in this restoration work. He designed much of the replacement stained glass for the church, as well as supervising the restoration of the long-lost Norman font. The Welsh poet Goronwy Owen was curate at St Mary's in the 18th century, and the neglected Liverpool architect Arthur Hill Holme lies buried in a large family tomb in the churchyard. He lies not far from the actor John Palmer, who died on stage at the Theatre Royal in 1798. The churchyard is leafy and attractive and has many old and fascinating graves, although as they are carved from sandstone many are crumbling and indecipherable. Vandalism too has taken its toll.

*Street lighting on a
wet night. Rice
Lane, 1960.*

At the time of the Domesday survey in 1086, the freemen of Walton were summoned to the Conqueror's tax assessors in West Derby to give an account of their township. This would include a list of property, owners, and the land's value. Liverpool is not mentioned in Domesday Book, but it is not impossible that (if it existed at all) the tiny fishing village was included in Walton's possessions. The township's influence was certainly strong at this time; it was a bigger township than West Derby, and Walton men owned land from Bootle to Toxteth.

In 1216 Henry III granted Walton a charter for a Tuesday market, and in the same century two large halls were built whose names still echo across the district today. Walton Hall Park is the truncated remains of the lands surrounding Walton Hall, which was already in existence by 1300. The remains of this house were discovered when the later Jacobean house was demolished after World War One. Spellow House stood on the site of modern Dane Street, off County Road, and was built by the Spellow family in approximately 1270. It stood near to a small hamlet called Mare Green, on modern Stanley Park. 'Spellow' is an ancient name, and Derek Whale argues that it is a corruption of an Anglo-Saxon name meaning 'Speech Hill', perhaps recording a local council meeting place; in which case the family could have taken their name from the location. The family were important local landowners and legend has it that Edward III stayed at Spellow House in 1341. There could also be a family connection with Spellow Mill, which stood near what would later be Barlow Lane in Kirkdale on possibly the old 'Speech Hill' itself. In the 18th and early 19th century Spellow Mill was a popular destination for local walks as it had views out to sea and across the river into Cheshire and Wales. The mill burned down in 1828, when it was rumoured to be at least 500 years old. It is possible that Spellow Lane, once the boundary between Walton and Kirkdale, was possibly 'the lane to Spellow hill'.

Spellow House survived to be inhabited in the 19th century by William Skirving, who is described as a 'seedsman' and ran a large nursery nearby. He moved out of the house into a new building, which became the first Spellow House Hotel, and the old Spellow House – then at least 600 years old – fell into decay. There was enough of it surviving in 1881 for it to be visited by local writer John Wilson, who recorded the building's final demolition not long afterwards. He also recorded the obscure Easter tradition of 'heaving' or 'lifting', common in Walton a century before. On Easter Monday the men of the town 'raced after the women, whom, having caught, they raised from the ground, the lifting sometimes accompanied by rough usage. The day following, the women assembled together and endeavoured to pay back with interest the lifting of the day before. No quarter was given to the men when captured...' The writer goes on to record with some Victorian satisfaction that 'the custom was a rude, indecent and dangerous one, and we are glad to find it relegated to the limbo of worthless things...'

When John Wilson was writing in the 1880s, Walton had been a small agricultural village for possibly a thousand years. There was increasing commerce with the improvement of the roads out of Liverpool and the coach road to Preston, but Wilson's century saw Walton transformed from a village to a suburb. William Forwood, looking back 60 years from 1910, wrote 'Walton was a very pretty village and remained so until a comparatively recent date; its lanes were shaded by stately trees amid which there nestled the charming old thatched cottages which formed the village.' But times were changing, and it was Forwood's generation that changed the face of Walton forever. Some old buildings were trampled in the rush, including the Guide House, on County Road. This was a single-storied thatched building used by guides who used their knowledge to lead travellers on foot across difficult or dangerous local terrain. This informal, nationwide network performed a valuable service in the years before stagecoaches, when people would walk from one part of the country to another as few could afford horses. The Guide House survived to be painted romantically by William Herdman, but was demolished in 1866 and a block of houses called Lauderdale Terrace was built on the site.

In the 80 years between 1801 and 1881, the population of Walton exploded from 700 to nearly 19,000, and the village became a suburb of the new city of Liverpool. In the late 19th century the district's main institutions were established. Walton Gaol was built between 1847 and 1855, and is still Liverpool's main prison today. The Irish Republican writer Brendan Behan was briefly incarcerated here, and wrote of his experiences in *Borstal Boy*. Quentin Hughes comments that John Weightman's original design was 'portentous castellated Norman', and adds dryly that the building is 'best seen from the outside'. Walton Hospital, now a centre of excellence in the treatment of brain damage, was built as a workhouse in 1868. Paul McCartney was born here in 1942, when the family was living in Walton. The Liverpool Zoological Gardens was established on a site later occupied by the Dunlop Rubber Company, and in 1851 the famous Walton Park Cemetery was laid out. The most famous inhabitant is Robert Noonan, who wrote *The Ragged-Trousered Philanthropists* under the name Robert Tressell. Noonan was born in Dublin, but died of tuberculosis in the Liverpool Royal Infirmary and was buried in 1911 in a pauper's grave, which was only marked by a gravestone in 1977. The

Hartley's jam factory, Long Lane, with Romany or fairground caravans on a field near the railway bridge. September, 1928.

artist James Carling is also buried in Walton. He was born on Scotland Road in 1858, and is supposed to have begun drawing by chalking on the pavement to raise money. He died in 1887 at the age of 29 after an unsuccessful career as an illustrator in the United States, but is today regarded as one of the best interpreters of the dark writings of Edgar Allen Poe.

Neat red-brick villas and terraced houses now cover much of Walton, and their building at the end of the 19th century completed the transition from rural village to suburb. John Moores's first Liverpool home was in one of these new houses, on Hahnemann Road, and it was at the kitchen table here that the first British football pools were worked out. Moores's family would collect the coupons by hand from matches in Liverpool and Manchester, and tally them on the kitchen table in Hahnemann Road. The house was certainly convenient for the football grounds, for Walton's border with Anfield is also the home of Everton Football Club, Goodison Park. Everton have been a football club since 1878, and are one of the oldest clubs

in the football league. The huge silver walls of the stadium dominate Goodison Road and the streets running to it from Walton Road, but the site is a difficult one for modern coaches and spectators' cars. At the time of writing there is talk of the club moving to a new purpose-built stadium further out from the city or even on the empty King's Dock site in the city centre. Facing the same problems, Liverpool FC are moving to new premises on Stanley Park. Everton are an institution here, and it would be a shame if the club left this 'north end' of the city altogether; their emblem is famously the old lockup in the empty centre of Everton Village, their nickname is the Toffees from the toffee shop that used to stand beside it, and their ground is in the very heart of north-end Liverpool. And for all the bustle Walton is not a wealthy suburb, and the presence of a major national football club brings much-needed income to local shops and pubs.

Walton was finally absorbed into Liverpool in 1895, when the fishing village took over the old township forever. Today it is a busy suburb of the city with a strong local identity, although more could be done to preserve the special nature of the heart of one of Liverpool's oldest lost villages.

Further reading

William Forwood, *Recollections of a Busy Life*, Liverpool, 1910.

Peter Howell Williams, *Liverpolitana*, 1971.

James Picton, *Memorials of Liverpool* Volume II, Liverpool, 1873.

Derek Whale, *Lost Villages of Liverpool* Part III, 1985.

John Wilson, *History of Walton*, Liverpool, 1891.

Fazakerley

This is the only place in England to bear this name, which could be Anglo-Saxon
and could mean 'the boundary near the field by the meadow'. For all the interest of
its name, Fazakerley has never been an attractive district. Murray's *Lancashire*
describes it bleakly as 'where Liverpool thins out inland to the north' and
emphasises this sense of empty hinterland still
further, by describing the 'isolation hospitals and
cemeteries, recreation grounds, children's Homes,
and the West Derby sewage farm…' For many
centuries Fazakerley was an agricultural district, but
the fields were described in 1907 as 'rather bare',
'extremely flat and treeless', and 'devoid of any beauty'. It had been farmed since
at least 1321, when the modern spelling was already being used, but a document
from 1333 calls the district 'Phesacrelegh', showing the rich variety available before
the language was standardised.

*Old Walton –
18th-century
graves in Walton
churchyard.*

Much of the history of the area before the 20th century revolves around the
Fazakerley family, who took their name from the district, and ran the manor of
Fazakerley for many centuries. The family had marriage connections with other
local landowners, such as the Moores at Bank Hall and the Molyneux at Croxteth.

*The Cottage
Homes,
Fazakerley, in
1957, with the
huge dining room
visible at the end
of the avenue.*

A side view of the ornate Prince Albert public house, County Road.

The Glebe Hotel, County Road. Walton has many attractive Victorian buildings.

They were Roman Catholic at the Reformation, and supported the King a century later in the Civil War. Nicholas Fazakerley died in 1643 in Liverpool supporting the Royalist cause. Much of their land was taken after the Civil War, and the family's fortunes began to wane. Their home, Fazakerley Hall, is long gone, but it stood off Longmoor Lane near Field Lane on the way to the modern M57.

Fazakerley has few buildings of interest, apart from the huge Cottage Homes. They are a series of semi-detached houses built along a broad avenue, and leading to the dining hall with a large clock tower, which is still a local landmark. The Homes were built between 1887 and 1889, at a time when Fazakerley was a long way out in the country from Liverpool, as a home for deprived children. Designed by Charles Lancaster, they had large safe gardens and a playing field for the children, and foster parents ran each house. The Homes closed down in 1958 and the site was converted into a mental health centre called New Hall, although the old name is still the most used.

The neighbouring district of Aintree has a history of settlement going back to the Anglo-Saxons, but is chiefly famous for one thing; the Grand National. The horse race has been run here since 1839, although the area was already used for steeple-chasing, and Derek Whale records the fact that the area was used for horse racing in the 16th century. Aintree is also famous locally for the factories along Long Lane, including the old Hartley's jam factory. William Hartley was a Victorian philanthropist who laid out a village for his workers and provided pensions and health care, at a time when such innovations were unheard of.

The site of Canon Lester's old church, Walton Road, now an attractive and peaceful garden.

The 'rather bare' fields of Fazakerley and Aintree were built over in the mid-20th century, when Fazakerley's huge housing estates were laid out. The flatness of the landscape made it ideal for large housing development, and Liverpool's first multi-storey tower block was built here in 1953, and appropriately called Coronation Court. The district has some attractive 20th-century churches and elegant tree-lined boulevards of housing, but Fazakerley is chiefly famous in Liverpool for its large hospital, which developed from an Isolation Hospital built here because of its distance from the city proper.

Further reading

Peter Fleetwood-Hesketh, *Murray's Guide to Lancashire*, 1955.
Derek Whale, *Lost Villages of Liverpool*, Parts II and III, 1985.
Victoria History of Lancashire Volume III, 1907.

Carving from the façade of Walton Town Hall, demolished for the widening of Queens Drive and preserved on a neglected corner of the modern road junction.

WAVERTREE AND WAVERTREE GARDEN SUBURB

It is possible that there has been a settlement at Wavertree for over 2,000 years. It has been suggested that Wavertree means 'a settlement near a spring on a wasteland', and could refer to a people settled near the old spring that later became known as the Monk's Well, but equally it could imply a place of waving trees, perhaps aspen. Other writers have detected Welsh or Cornish echoes in the name, and their suggestion of an ancient British settlement was borne out in 1867 when a small cemetery of prehistoric urn burials was discovered on Olive Mount. The urns are now in the vaults of Liverpool Museum, having escaped the fate of their prehistoric neighbour, whose grave became the Calderstones. It is possible that the settlement was clustered around the spring at the Monk's Well, and that Wavertree at the time was heath or thin woods, perhaps of the 'wavy trees'. The low hill that

Wavertree Lake in May 1957, now the site of the playground near the lock-up.

became Olive Mount could have been used for a cemetery because it was the highest point locally, or perhaps a boundary between 'tribes'. This is supposition, but what is certain is that there were people living and burying their dead here before the Romans came to Britain.

For many centuries Wavertree was agricultural, a patchwork landscape of fields and small woods, but it also had its own mill and quarry. Wavertree Mill was built in the mid-1400s, and stood on the small rise of Charles Berrington Road and Beverley Road. Behind it, facing modern Woolton Road, was a small quarry, which for many years provided stone to the people of Wavertree before being filled in the 1920s. The road to the mill, which would have overlooked the quarry, is still there. It serves as a cut-through from Woolton Road to Charles Berrington Road, but the mill itself was closed in 1889 and demolished in 1916. A plaque on the houses on the site records its position.

The small village of Wavertree was strung out along 'Wavertree Lane', modern Wavertree Road, which connected it with other small places such as the hamlet near Vernon Hall that would grow into Edge Hill. Wavertree also stood on the edge of Childwall Heath, and was connected by winding farm tracks with the nearby hamlets of Allerton and Childwall. Many of these tracks were straightened and

A shelter for tram crews on the junction of Smithdown Road and Ullet Road, in March 1899.

The Grand Cinema, Smithdown Road, in 1961, before road improvements.

levelled at the end of the 18th century, when it was realised that some of them were hundreds if not thousands of years old. In 1731 there were 290 people living in Wavertree, and the township had 60 houses in it; but the village was changing dramatically at this time. Improved roads brought the town of Liverpool within easy reach, and old villages such as Everton and Wavertree became popular places to build country houses. The rich needed houses for their servants, who needed shops and inns; by 1801 there were 860 houses in the township, and records show that in 1811 1,400 people lived here.

There are still a handful of 18th-century buildings today near the old village green, in the oldest surviving part of the village. Famously the local hunt used to meet here, on the edge of what was then open country. The lock-up opposite was built in the late 18th century to house drunks, as in addition to the hunt many people came to find Wavertree a popular place to drink. In later life the lock-up was also used for cholera victims – the dead and the living – and as temporary accommodation for homeless Irish families driven from Ireland by the Famine. The lock-up outlived its usefulness as long ago as 1852.

Picton Clock in 1897.

Wavertree Mill, photographed in February 1909 in a very poor condition. It was demolished in 1916.

Wavertree has strong links with James Picton, the antiquarian, architect, and author. Picton is one of the great writers of Liverpool's history, and came to live here in the mid-19th century. He built the famous Picton Clock in memory of his wife, and the main road through the village also bears his name. There are so many references that the area could almost be called Picton. The family lived at Sandy Knowe on Mill Lane, which would then have been running through open countryside, and is still standing, although much altered. Earlier in the century, the poet Felicia Hemans lived on Wavertree High Street. She had been born in Liverpool, and returned, after living in North Wales, to live here between 1828 and 1831. She is most remembered today for her poem *Casabianca,* with its famous (and much-parodied) opening line 'The boy stood on the burning deck...' Her house was demolished in 1958. (At about the same time George Harrison lived with his family in Arnold Grove, although less than five years later the success of the Beatles meant that he left Liverpool for ever, and moved the family out to a new house near Warrington.)

The imposing Abbey Cinema in 1939. It is now a supermarket.

In common with many of the old villages that make up modern suburban Liverpool, the Victorians destroyed Wavertree's rural character. In 1851 Wavertree became a local government district, with the Town Hall being built 20 years later. It still stands, on Picton Road, painted gaudily and now a pub-restaurant, and still has its civic motto, *Sub umbra floresco*, 'I flourish in the shade'. But the shade was darkening; the Victorians built many streets of red-brick terraced housing and turned a semi-rural village into a suburb. In 1894 Wavertree became an urban district, but even so it was still on the edge of open country, although the land towards Childwall and Allerton was by then farmland and not the heath land it had once been. Its large parks and the Botanic Gardens preserved Wavertree's rural character. In 1836, the gardens had moved to the land between Wavertree Road and Edge Lane. This had once been the site of Wavertree Hall, and was the home of the Botanic Gardens until bomb damage during World War Two forced the move out to Calderstones Park.

Ancient Wavertree; old windows in the heart of the village.

The most famous of Wavertree's parks today is Wavertree Playground, popularly known as the Mystery. Philip Holt of the shipping firm donated this large park to the city in 1895, the year that Wavertree officially became part of Liverpool. For many years the donor's identity was unknown, hence the name. The park was once farmland, and occasionally the old lanes reappear, echoes of Georgian Wavertree, marked by darker grass in dry summers.

Wavertree was now officially a suburb and had over 25,000 inhabitants in 1901, and nearly three times that by 1947. The city laid out roads of fine semi-detached houses among the old Victorian mansions and small parks of villas, and the suburb acquired the look it has today, a mixture of old and new, cheek by jowl.

Modern Wavertree has a good collection of historic buildings. The lock-up was built in the 1780s, Holy Trinity church dates from 1794, and there are still Georgian houses near the old pubs of the Lamb and the Coffee House. It has fine 20th-century buildings too; the old Technology College, the swimming baths, and the library, which is inevitably named after James Picton, form a collection of civic buildings on busy Picton Road. The grand 'Queen Anne Baroque' in terracotta and sandstone of the Bluecoat School sits on a fine site dominating the Mystery. At the

Crumbling and insanitary property on Hills Place in 1934.

The Lamb public house, Wavertree, one of the district's oldest pubs.

end of the 20th century Wavertree opened a technology park, to give employment to an area left bereft by the loss of the big factories that used to employ hundreds of people along Edge Lane.

Enough of Wavertree's history has been preserved to keep the echoes of the rural village it once was, although the High Street is now a busy route into and out of the city, and is never quiet. It is a shame that the prehistoric burial urns are no longer here, but enough has survived in Wavertree to keep the past very close to the present.

Wavertree Garden Suburb

Liverpool Garden Suburb is important enough in the local context to warrant a chapter to itself. It grew out of the Garden Cities movement of the early 20th century, when it began to be realised that it was possible to combine the best of town and country, the convenience of the city with the peacefulness of the countryside and the community life of a village. The amount of housing in an area was kept low and the houses were well spaced, with large gardens and roads which were deliberately winding and tree-lined, to create views of houses peeping from behind hedges and trees, an idyll of country life in the city.

Liverpool Garden Suburb was begun in 1912, when the first cottages were built between Thingwall Road and Queens Drive. There were already pockets of middle-class housing in the area, in the almost forgotten areas of Olive Vale and Wavertree Nook, and city engineer John Brodie was connecting existing roads to form the

Wavertree Garden Suburb with its generous gardens and idyllic country atmosphere.

huge Queens Drive, Liverpool's first ring road, but much of this part of Wavertree was still semi-rural. The new Garden Suburb was built around existing roads, with Heywood Road, Wavertree Nook Road and Thingwall Road providing a skeleton for the new district. In keeping with good Garden Cities practice the houses were similar but individual, in short terraces, semi-detached or detached, but very similar one to another. There were hedges and trees planted, and large areas given over to grass. The opening was celebrated with Morris dancing and village events, and there was much talk of 'open-air parliaments' and talks and events on the village greens. The beginning of World War One saw a slowing and a halt to the building programme, however, and as the war dragged on the grand plan was never realised. Less than a quarter of the planned garden suburb was built, and the planned extension across Queens Drive – intended to run through the estate – never materialised. This is perhaps why it has seemed such a local development, why it has always been known as Wavertree Garden Suburb. But it is also perhaps why the garden suburb has retained its village atmosphere; any bigger and it would have felt more like a suburb proper. Much that was temporary became permanent, such as areas for shops or the Garden Suburb Institute on Thingwall Road, both of which were only intended to provide for the area until it was finished.

In 1974 the City Council declared the Garden Suburb a conservation area, which preserved its appearance for the future and ensured that it is still an interesting area to walk around today. The area has neat paths through the estate, clipped or shaggy hedges, large grassy fields, and passageways connecting winding roads and open spaces. There are a lot of trees, and a sense of quiet; boys on bikes and birdsong, although the suburb was not designed for today's car ownership. After 90 years the planting has reached maturity, and the pathways give glimpses of small gardens and pleasant white cottages through the hedges.

Further reading

Mike Chitty, *Walking Historic Wavertree*, Liverpool, 1999.
Colin Gould, *A Pictorial History of Wavertree*, Liverpool, 1983.
James Hoult, *West Derby, Old Swan and Wavertree*, Liverpool, 1913.
J.A. Maw, *Wavertree – A Chronicle*, Liverpool, c.1978.
Liverpool City Council, Wavertree Garden Suburb leaflet, Liverpool, 1974.
George Rose, *Garden City Ideals*, paper read at 'The City Beautiful' conference, Liverpool, 1907.

WEST DERBY

West Derby was an important township when Liverpool was a small muddy fishing port on the banks of an obscure river. The district was heavily wooded, and the forest of West Derby was used for hunting; the name itself might suggest this, as *deor* (Anglo-Saxon) or *dyr* (Norse) could refer to a wild animal (the source of our word 'deer') and *by* (a common word in many Scandinavian languages) suggests a township, but it is equally possible that it was named after a person; 'Deor's town'.

West Derby was the centre of a Hundred, which stretched along the shoreline from 'North Meols' above modern Southport to Warrington, and across to Wigan and Ormskirk. One theory is that the Hundreds were districts capable of raising 100 fighting men. Lancashire at the time was divided into only six Hundreds; in comparison Norfolk had 33, which shows how sparsely populated the county was at the time. The Vikings arrived in West Derby in the 9th century, and added an extra layer of bureaucracy with the Wapentake, or 'weapon-touch'. These are the distant ancestors of the modern County Court system, but in addition to dealing with debts, tenures, and land issues, the touching of weapons was a sign of allegiance to the king.

West Derby's importance as the centre of the Hundred and the Wapentake is underlined in its name; it is West Derby to distinguish it from Derby in the Midlands. For many centuries, West Derby was important enough to merit a castle, which before the Normans was probably a wooden structure surrounded by a ditch. The Normans built a larger castle here on their 'motte and bailey' principle, which until recently was clearly visible from the air as shadows on the fields. The castle was allowed to decay as the area declined in importance after King John's decision to found Liverpool, and was eventually demolished and cleared. Castle Green, a landscaped park in the ocean of 1930s suburbia that now surrounds the old village, marks the site. The decline in importance had begun as long ago as the 13th century, when King John transferred the Wapentake Court to Liverpool.

For many centuries West Derby was a landscape of farmland and woods, dotted with large private houses in substantial grounds. The smaller houses of the servants and farm labourers were in the village itself, clustered around the entrance to the huge Croxteth Park. This is the park surrounding Croxteth Hall, one of north Liverpool's greatest public parks. Part of the old house dates back to the 16th

century, but most of the present building was built in the grandiose manner of the late 17th and early 18th century. The Hall was for many centuries the home of the Molyneux family, one of the great families of the area, who owned or controlled huge swathes of Liverpool and had a great deal of involvement in her history. (Over centuries the Molyneux vied with the Stanleys to become Liverpool's premier family, the Montagues and the Capulets of north western England.) Croxteth Hall and its huge grounds are now owned by the City Council, and it is maintained as a civic amenity, a large country park open to all free of charge.

James Hoult records the old Easter tradition of 'Pase-Egging' in south-west Lancashire, but especially in Wavertree and West Derby. He was writing in the 1930s but recalling a tradition 'which was observed up to forty years ago'. By then, however, 'it had degenerated into a play performed by bands of boys dressed up with coloured ribbons, with tinsel and paper caps, and armed with wooden or tin swords.' The Pase-Egging show was a form of Mummers' Play, with characters such as St George, the Black Moroccan King, the Doctor and Beelezebub. St George was the hero and routed various enemies who were then healed by the Doctor, and 'the play, as the stories and plays of those days usually did, finished happily, all joining in a dance.' Hoult says that the Pase-Eggers of West Derby 'were esteemed to be the best in the district around Liverpool, Wavertree coming a close second.'

This rural West Derby of large houses and village cottages was transformed in the mid-20th century, when many miles of roads of neat, semi-detached houses were built. The district has pockets of older buildings such as Sandfield Park, on the border with Queens Drive and Stoneycroft, which is a leafy estate of large, crumbling, sandstone houses in the Italianate style; but most that is interesting is in the heart of the old village itself, around the gates of Croxteth Park. Despite its long history, modern West Derby has no buildings dating from before the 17th century, with the old courthouse of 1662 and Yeoman's Cottage from roughly 60 years earlier. Modern West Derby is a bustling and lively village, with a large number of pubs, and some shops and restaurants. There is a great deal here for visitors; the old buildings of the village, Croxteth Hall, the huge St Mary's church designed by George Gilbert Scott, and the rural open space of Croxteth Park. At the time of writing it is also possible that the Casbah Club will reopen as a tourist attraction. This small Merseybeat club was opened in the late 1950s in the basement of her house by Mona Best, the mother of Pete Best, the first Beatles drummer. But all too often Liverpool does not make the most of its assets, and far more could be done to celebrate the long history and individuality of this area.

Further reading

J.G. Cooper and A.D. Power, *A History of West Derby*, Causeway Books, 1982.

James Hoult, *West Derby, Old Swan, and Wavertree*, Liverpool, 1913.

Kay Parrott, *West Derby and Norris Green*, 1996.

Derek Whale, *Lost Villages of Liverpool* Part II, 1985.

The old courthouse, West Derby village, photographed in 1934 when it was the headquarters of the local Conservative party.

WOOLTON

Woolton is the most famous of Liverpool's urban villages, although the modern suburb is far bigger than the village centre. It runs from Black Woods and the border with Childwall and Allerton, to Halewood and Hunts Cross, but the heart of the district is the old village. It is an Old Norse or Anglo Saxon name, meaning 'Wulf's enclosure', the farmstead created by a man named Wulf or Ulf, a common Scandinavian name. It is probable, however, that Wulf found a settlement already here. It has been argued that Camp Hill was occupied, and defended by ramparts, before the Romans came to Britain, and the date of 150 BC has been mentioned. The Hill is a ridge some 250 feet high, and would certainly be a good site for perhaps a fortified farmhouse or small village, as it sits on the top of the hill with excellent views down to the river and across the Wirral into Wales. The Scandinavians would

have had as much use for the site as the Iron Age people who created it, and it is probable that the first Woolton village was on Camp Hill. Wulf's name echoes in the Domesday records of Woolton and Gateacre, which are mentioned as Ulvetune and Uvetone respectively.

From 1178 the Knights Hospitallers, an order of monks who cared for sick pilgrims, owned the area. It is possible that they erected the series of roadside crosses that marked the road from Speke to Childwall church, although only the rebuilt crosses at Hunts Cross, Woolton, and Childwall Lane survive today. Their lands were seized by the Crown when Henry VIII dissolved the monasteries in the 1540s, although for many years after it was compulsory for Woolton residents to have a cross set upon their houses, a relic of the time when the manor was controlled by the Hospitallers. The manor was sold on at the beginning of the 17th century, and Woolton was acquired by Isaac Greene, the Liverpool lawyer who invested heavily in land, and through his female descendants passed into the hands of the Marquis of Salisbury.

The land is not particularly fertile, but Woolton has been a rural village for most of its history. In 1658 there were only 175 inhabitants, but there had been enough children to need a school since the early part of the century. The old schoolhouse on School Lane is dated 1610, but the school's true founding date remains a mystery. There are many references to it in wills and records from the 17th century, and the Catholic martyr St John Almond declared in his trial of 1612 that he was educated at a school in Woolton; it is possible that this is the same establishment. There is certainly some mystery about the little building. 'Some authorities believe that originally it was a pre-Reformation chapel,' writes Derek Whale. 'It has also served as a cottage, cowshed and barn.' With a pleasant historical symmetry, the school is now a pre-school nursery after some years of dereliction.

It is possible that Woolton Hall was also in existence at this time. The present 1704 building is possibly built around a far older structure, perhaps dating back to the 1560s. Woolton Hall is supposed to include the only work in Lancashire by Robert Adam, but architectural historian Quentin Hughes is dismissive, criticising its 'unsatisfactory mishmash of parts, some ill-proportioned and not coming together to form a whole.' The Hall was built for the Molyneux family, but it is now a pub/restaurant next to the modern St Julie's school.

Woolton's population exploded in numbers in the 19th century. There were 439 inhabitants in 1801, but over 4,500 by the end of the century. There are a number of reasons for this. After the Childwall and Woolton Waste Lands Enclosure Act of

Woolton village on a sunny day in July 1957. Very little has changed apart from the amount of traffic.

1805 the local gentry, who needed labourers to build walls and fences and work their new property, enclosed much of the common land. Some enclosed land became agricultural, but Woolton has rocky soil and it was more profitable to exploit the stone as building material. This led to the development of small quarries all over the district. Woolton Quarry was opened by James Rose, known as the King of Woolton, who was responsible for the district's regeneration in the 19th century. He built many houses for both rich and poor, and reclaimed Woolton Heath for housing. He is remembered in Rose Place and Rose Brow, which were streets built by him with rows of cottages. His quarry was a local source of stonework for Liverpool's wealthy who began building here, and their houses in turn required large numbers of servants. The quarry's stone built many local buildings, and eventually the huge Liverpool Cathedral. It is now closed, and modern semi-detached houses have been built in its huge maw, with tiny hanging baskets screwed to the great walls.

The population of Woolton also rose because of the huge numbers of Irish people who fled the Great Famine and settled all over Liverpool. In 1851 an incredible 24 percent of Woolton's population had been born in Ireland, and many worked on the new docks and railway system at Garston. Ale was relatively cheap, and with over

40 pubs in Woolton in the 1870s, the stonecutters and dock navvies had a reputation for disorderly and drunken behaviour. The main duty of the police in Woolton at this time was to patrol the grounds of the wealthy to prevent burglary or drunken insurrection.

Life was hard for the poor in Woolton in the middle decades of the 19th century. They lived in terraces of small cottages, on Rose Street, Rodick Street and Quarry Street, and Kay Parrott comments that 'many people had exchanged rural poverty for urban poverty.' In the harsh winter of 1874 a soup kitchen was established, which fed 450 people twice a day for 11 days at a cost of £40. But many Woolton houses at the end of the century grew vegetables, and the village was famous for the quality of its pigs. Parrott comments that Woolton's poor were probably better off than those in central Liverpool, as they were nearer the countryside and fewer in number.

In 1913 Woolton became part of Liverpool, and over the next 50 years it lost much of its individuality, as the fields between Woolton, Gateacre and Allerton

Woolton Street and the Cross in 1960, before the demolition of the old houses.

were built over with houses. The 1930s saw many miles of semi-detached houses being built in Allerton and Woolton, and in one of these John Lennon lived for much of his early life. He attended summertime concerts in the grounds of Strawberry Fields, a Salvation Army home on Beaconsfield Road; bright new buildings have replaced the sombre Victorian house, but the old ornate red gates are still a Beatles shrine. His home on Menlove Avenue has been recently donated to the National Trust by Yoko Ono, and restored to the style of the 1950s, as has Paul McCartney's house in Allerton. Paul himself was a chorister in the church of St Peter, on Church Road. The sculptor Arthur Dooley, another figure from the Liverpool art scene of the early 1960s, had a studio and bar in the Bodega, on Quarry Street. Woolton has a higher number of pubs than many other similar-sized areas of the city, an indication of the density of population in the poorest areas in the 19th century.

Modern Woolton has interesting Victorian buildings and pubs, one of the few independent cinemas in the city, good restaurants, old pubs and new bars, and some smart shops. The village was declared a conservation area in 1969 and new developments are very low key. Woolton today is a wealthy suburb, with the desirable sandstone cottages in the urban village heart surrounded by wide roads of large semi-detached properties; but it is still near the open green space of Camp Hill, Clarke's Gardens, and Allerton golf course, which together with the attractive village heart, help to keep alive the mood of the village's rural past.

Further reading

John E. Lally, and, Janet B. Gnosspelius, *History of Much Woolton*, The Woolton Society, 1975.

The Townswomen's Guild, *History of Much Woolton*, private publication.

Derek Whale, *Lost Villages of Liverpool* Part II, 1985.

Woolton Ordnance Survey map 1904, notes by Kay Parrott, Alan Godfrey Maps.

VERTICAL SUBURBS

In recent years the pattern of suburban building has changed in Liverpool. The green belt has stopped further outward expansion, and developers have been forced to build small estates in between older housing, filling in the gaps of dereliction, neglect or bomb damage. More recently, the city's skyline has been changed as developers have built tall glass tower blocks in the city centre, just as the last of the 1960s tower blocks have been decommissioned. The creation of these new 'vertical suburbs' in the city centre is inseparable from the process of urban regeneration that the city has been going through since the 1980s, and rightly or wrongly they have set the tone for a new approach to urban and suburban building in the city.

For the first 500 years of its history, Liverpool had no suburbs. The mediaeval population lived in the town centre behind high walls, probably made of mud brick, which were only cleared in the 1600s. Inside the walls, the original seven streets of the city had everything a

Yorkshire House, Tithebarn Street.

citizen could need: shops, churches, warehouses, inns, houses. There was no separation of work and home; everything happened on the same street, the same plot. Vegetables were grown on common-ground plots behind the buildings, and animals were grazed on heathland just beyond the walls on Dale Street. However, in the early 1700s, as the population grew and military technology made brick walls obsolete, the town council began to encourage speculative builders to develop the marshy land over the Pool, the tidal creek that is now marked by Whitechapel and Paradise Street. The gentle slope up from the Pool along Church and Bold Street is still recognisable as the landscape laid out by these Georgian builders. Williamson and Clayton Squares are no longer suburban, as the city's centre has grown with the outward expansion of the city, but they were built as 'sub-urban' development away

*Old and new,
Tithebarn Street.*

from Liverpool's industry and the shipbuilding on the Pool. This gradual expansion was the way the town grew over the next two centuries. The first developers were rich Liverpool merchants, who built themselves mansions and laid out estates in Aigburth, Everton or Kensington. They wanted the peace and quiet of the countryside but needed to be within easy reach of their businesses and social lives in the town centre. They were followed by speculative builders who transformed the same areas into suburbs. The 'inner city' villages or small settlements at Everton, Kirkdale, Wavertree and Vauxhall are still dotted with the ghosts or memories of the mansions that once stood there, but in most cases the village or 'pre-suburb' has disappeared completely. Only much further from the city centre has some sense of rural suburban life been retained, for example in Childwall, Woolton or Garston, where old village hearts have not been obliterated and where it was decided to enhance the village atmosphere and not build over it. The Victorians accelerated this process considerably, and in 50 years the farmland around Liverpool disappeared under rows of neat streets.

In the 20th century the city expansion reached its height. The council built huge suburbs around the city as part of its ongoing slum-clearance programme and after World War Two rehoused people in new towns at Runcorn and Skelmersdale, towns which have their own identity and problems and are not really suburbs of Liverpool at all, despite originally being populated by Liverpudlians. The quality of the roads improved considerably, and more organised transport – first horse-drawn trams, then electric trams and suburban railways, and finally an extensive bus network and wider ownership of cars – made it possible to live in the peace and quiet of the suburbs but work in the city centre. This pattern of suburban growth was repeated across the country as Britain's old cities coped with the pressures of 19th and 20th-century commercial and technological development, and massive growth.

The mentality behind these 300 years of 'suburbanisation', the ideal of a three-storey townhouse in a quiet square or a semi-detached house with a small leafy garden, saw the city as somewhere to escape from, a place only visited because of need, mainly work. This was possibly a folk-memory of the cramped and unhygienic conditions before cities began to expand beyond ancient boundaries, but for the middle classes in particular the city was associated with poverty and violence, crime and disease for many years. Once suburban living became possible it was largely the working classes who stayed in the city, those housed by the council, but these quiet communities are still here, and today new developments sit next to far older municipal housing in districts such as Vauxhall or new suburban areas such as Ropewalks. It was attitudes among richer people – homeowners – that began to change towards the end of the 1980s, when living in the city centre began to be seen as desirable and fashionable.

Old and new, Duke Street.

There were established international patterns for this new mood of urban living which had been developed by cities as diverse as Amsterdam or New York. In Britain the new urban lifestyles have been created for wealthy young people, but in America it was unemployed people and artists who took over the empty city-centre warehouses and converted them into homes or 'lofts'. In New York the process was supposedly started by squatters, artists and soldiers returning from the war in 1945 unable to afford suburban property prices, but who, in any case, no longer wanted or believed in the older suburban ideal. They saw the city as exciting and vibrant, not as a place of danger, or perhaps the suggestion of danger gave city

*Old and new on
Pall Mall.*

living a piquancy that suburban living did not have. The new approach chimed well with post-war restlessness and energy, and in Liverpool redundant fruit warehouses on Mathew Street were occupied and transformed in the 1970s by squatters and imaginative artists, who began the psychological transformation of this area into the Cavern Quarter – the car-free district of bars, shops and art galleries that it is today. This punk spirit did not spread, however, and in the UK generally the process did not begin until the mid-1980s, with the massive regeneration of London's docklands. Rotting wharfs, crumbling warehouses and whole streets of the dockside East End were rebuilt and renovated into micro-villages and new homes in the city centre, and the perspective of the business district was shifted by the development of the gigantic Canary Wharf scheme and its associated projects. This scheme could only have been put into place by a huge city as it required massive infrastructure change, new railway lines and colossal investment, but other British cities took the lead on a smaller scale and began to look at empty warehouses and factories to convert into new homes and business premises.

In Liverpool the 1980s was the end of an era. The old Victorian port, whose city-centre businesses revolved around insurance, shipping and the docks, finally ran out of steam. New industries such as the huge car plant at Halewood seemed too subject to international pressures to bring permanent prosperity. Businesses and people had been leaving since the end of World War Two and Liverpool had an unenviable reputation for poverty and unemployment. The city was rundown and physically crumbling, and a misguided attempt by a left-wing city council to politically challenge Conservative central government added to the city's malaise by knocking business confidence still further and damaging the city's reputation.

It could be argued that the process of regeneration back from this gloomy decay began in Liverpool after the disturbances in Toxteth, when the poverty and lack of opportunities available became more widely known, but a number of factors fell into place at about the same time to enable the city's rehabilitation. A new generation of city councillors learned from their predecessors' mistakes and looked at successful cities such as Manchester, which combined strong local government with a willingness to work with the private sector. The deregulation of higher education allowed Liverpool Polytechnic to spread its wings and become Liverpool John Moores University, with a sharp increase in student numbers (not many of whom wanted to live in the suburbs) and more money freed to spend on buildings. The clubbing culture spawned new bars and restaurants and investment in the city centre, which indirectly led to a need for urban homes. Smaller businesses replaced the traditional Liverpool industries, and new service industries or IT and film concerns slowly began to take the place of shipping, the docks and car manufacture, a painful and bloody process which was not without its casualties. The transition

Chapel Street.

was as much emotional and spiritual as physical or topographical and has taken Liverpool in a radical new direction. Arguably it culminated in the city's year as European Capital of Culture, although the planned physical regeneration of the city will take many more years to complete.

Central government in the early 1980s took no interest in the inner cities, however, and it took the riots in the summer of 1981, especially in Liverpool and Bristol, for them to realise how rundown many of the country's inner cities had become. The national government responded by appointing Michael Heseltine to investigate the problems, and he became popularly known as 'minister for Merseyside'. His flamboyance, integrity and high-profile approach gradually attracted new investment and businesses to Liverpool, but the most obvious outcome of his work was the International Garden Festival in 1984. The industrial shore-front between Otterspool and the end of the south docks at Herculaneum Dock had been derelict and decaying for many years, but it was transformed into a

A pattern of girders, Dock Road.

vibrant tourist attraction by landscaping it with hundreds of trees and grassland and attracting garden designs from all over the world. A temporary ferry terminal was opened and the Mersey Ferries ran between Otterspool and the Pier Head. A narrow-gauge railway ran through the gardens, amphitheatres and stages saw performances by groups of Liverpool schoolchildren and dancers from all over the world, and the landscape was dotted with colourful and popular sculpture. The city was also given a huge and elegant modern performance venue called the Festival Arena, which to the city's shame lay derelict for many years before being demolished in 2007. It was intended that much of the festival site would be redeveloped afterwards for new housing, almost a new suburb, although only a small percentage has been built over, and this in a very traditional pattern of modern streets and pastiche houses. Much of the site has since run wild, with peeling 1980s sculpture standing forlorn in groves of young trees, and the paths overgrown and only used by dog walkers. Even at the time, the festival was seen as a mixed blessing by the city, and many people felt that no amount of tree-planting was going to halt the decline of a sea port and bring back the thousands of jobs that had been lost since 1945.

However, the International Garden Festival could be said to be the beginning of the city's modern life, and the start of its current mentality. This was the first time that Liverpool had imagined itself as a tourist attraction, the first time that it saw its architectural and historical assets as attractive and commercial, the first steps on the road to the city seeing itself as a provider of entertainment, university education and holiday accommodation; as a provider of service industries rather than the traditional industries of shipping and manufacture. Perhaps it is no coincidence that this new mood began to be reflected in new housing. At the same time as the festival was being developed, and perhaps because of Heseltine's work on the River Mersey, developers began to look again at the city centre and in particular the Albert Dock.

The Albert Dock had been built by Jesse Hartley in the 1840s and was ground-breaking in its design and method of dock working. Hartley isolated the Albert Dock from the Dock Road to prevent theft and corruption. He built a dock basin with a sturdy Italianate colonnade of fire-proof iron and brick warehouses, which did not even burn during the Blitz, a century after they opened. But for all its technological advances it has been estimated that the dock was obsolete only a decade after completion, and by the time of World War Two it was far too small for the large container

Leeds-Liverpool Canal buildings, Old Hall Street.

vessels of the time. By the 1980s the graceful buildings were derelict and empty, there was 15ft of mud and silt in the basin and the cobbled quays were overgrown with weeds, their capstans rusted and rotting. The Albert Dock is the largest collection of Grade I listed buildings in the country (outside London), and with the dawning awareness of the importance and possibilities of 'heritage' it was felt that this asset was crumbling into the river. So the basin was drained of mud, the bomb damage was invisibly repaired and the floors of arched-brick vaulting were converted into the city's first 'luxury apartments', which gave new residents fantastic soft views of the silver waters of the Mersey and the distant spires and towers of Birkenhead. The ground floor overlooking the dock basin, where the cargoes were once unloaded, was given over to shops and tourist attractions,

Stanley Dock, still undeveloped.

restaurants and bars. A number of 'anchor tenants' (high-profile businesses prepared to commit to the site for a long time) were persuaded to move into the new development, such as Granada TV and the *This Morning* TV show, which floated a famous weather map of the UK in the basin for their weatherman Fred Talbot. The key note in this regeneration was attracting the Tate Gallery to the Albert Dock, and a series of exhibitions by some of the giants of 20th-century art (perhaps deliberately controversial giants) such as Mark Rothko and Salvador Dali grabbed local headlines and polarised opinion – and helped to seal the new Tate and the Albert Dock in the city's imagination and the awareness of the country.

The Albert Dock was the first attractive but derelict building in Liverpool to be converted to modern luxury accommodation, but others followed. The city has seven miles of docklands fronting the river, and in the mood of the times these were the obvious first place for redevelopment on the London model. After 20 years as the city's biggest free car park and the venue for the Summer Pops concerts, the King's Dock has new apartment blocks and the long-awaited water-front stadium, although this cannot be said to be a successful arrangement. The old sheds of Brunswick Dock were torn down and replaced by a 'fishing village' of small new houses around the quays. The Liverpool Marina moved into the old Coburg Dock, and Toxteth Dock was drained and filled and became a small business park, the long sheds being redeveloped into relatively small units. The south docks terminate at the Herculaneum Dock, which was cleared some years ago, but a recent development of apartments around a remodelled stretch of water has emerged just a stone's throw from the end of the old Garden Festival site. North of the Pier Head the story is less clear. The Waterloo Dock buildings, taller and more solid but less impressive than the Albert Dock, were converted into luxury accommodation, but the docklands regeneration ends there, and the miles of docks beyond – Clarence, Trafalgar, even the Jesse Hartley project of Stanley Dock – lie derelict, as overgrown and rusty as they were 20 years ago. Attempts to attract the city's new money to Vauxhall have been only partially successful. Perhaps there are limits to the city's capacity for luxury waterfront accommodation, or perhaps limits to the civic idea of regeneration itself; or perhaps the time is just not right, and in 20 years the docks will have been rejuvenated with a mixture of shipping and accommodation, work and play, from Herculaneum to the enormous Freeport at Seaforth, creating a linear strip of modern city, a huge new waterfront 'suburb'.

Redundant buildings across the city were also remodelled as both apartments and shops, such as the empty Victorian post

Victoria Street Post Office, remodelled as the Met Quarter.

office between Victoria Street and Whitechapel, which after over 30 years of lying empty and roofless has been sand-blasted and re-roofed and is now the elegant Met Quarter shopping mall. The famous Liverpool Collegiate School on Shaw Street has been transformed from derelict shell to bright urban apartments. The Collegiate was designed by Harvey Lonsdale Elmes, the architect of St George's Hall, with deliberate echoes of the great English schools founded at the Reformation, and its conversion by the development company Urban Splash has saved this important piece of Liverpool's architectural history. The old St Francis Xavier School across the road is the new home for Hope University College. This used to be the Liverpool Institute for Higher Education, which modernised and expanded on the Liverpool Polytechnic model, and their partial transference to Shaw Street has kick-started a small pattern of redevelopment. One development gives confidence to others, and the combination in Everton of the Collegiate, the fine SFX Church and Hope University has attracted other developers to look at the Baptist chapel over the road and the fine but derelict Georgian town houses on Shaw Street. These four-storey houses are well-positioned on the slope of Everton Brow, and with post-war clearances most have unrivalled views down through old industrial Everton and Vauxhall to the distant city centre. Indeed some of these attractive buildings have already been saved and converted and make elegant city homes, as do their sister town houses in the old red-light district of Liverpool 8, which are now renovated and once again worth huge sums of money. The old Ear and Eye Hospital on Myrtle Street, with its terracotta Gothic detailing and overhanging roofline, has been reborn as the Symphony building, so named as it stands opposite the Philharmonic Hall. The elegant Women's Hospital on Catherine Street has been redeveloped to provide student housing, with the car parking hidden in well-landscaped grounds. The grandest of these projects is the regeneration of the gigantic North Western Hotel, designed by the Liverpool architect Alfred Waterhouse as a hotel complex attached to Lime Street Station. Waterhouse was a giant of late-Victorian architecture, who designed the Natural History Museum in London as well as Manchester Town Hall and many buildings for the Prudential Assurance Company. He also designed large private houses, including one in a quiet part of Allerton which has been stylishly converted to apartments. The North Western Hotel was empty for many years, until it was redeveloped by Liverpool John Moores University to provide student accommodation, with bars and eating places on the ground floor.

The new mood of confidence in the city centre led to the conversion of old attractive properties and the building of new apartments on 'brownfield' sites, but there came a point where there was not enough old property to satisfy the demands of property developers and new buildings were called for. Many new developments were carefully designed to fit into the existing urban landscape such as Queen Square, which almost invisibly mended a gash in the city fabric and replaced an ugly car park with restaurants and bars, a hotel and a large car park well-designed as a mock-warehouse. But around the millennium year the city began to have the confidence to build housing on a larger scale, and very tall apartment blocks in steel and glass began to appear in the city centre, changing Liverpool's skyline. Their names commemorate the city's mercantile and maritime past, they are called 'wharves', 'quays' and 'warehouses', but from across the river the city's familiar

*Murky skyline –
Liverpool from
Birkenhead, 2008.*

landmarks are dwarfed by the new buildings, and the new skyline is not a particularly attractive one.

In 2004 Liverpool achieved World Heritage Site status because of the international importance of its waterfront buildings and urban landscape, but UNESCO, the body behind world heritage sites, are uneasy about the towers' impact on the cityscape. They are too geographically spread out to provide a new urban cluster, an inner city of towers, and do not provide ambitious architectural statements in their own right, seeming to rely on size to be impressive. They erupt awkwardly from the low skyline and create the impression of urban sprawl. They have changed the dynamic of the narrow streets around them, especially in the old Georgian and Victorian business district of Old Hall Street, where they display an arrogant disregard for the landscape and streetscape they have been built into. The older business buildings were built of brick, stone and stucco and have weathered gracefully over the decades. The new towers are made of glass and metal, which clash harshly with the generous materials of the older buildings. They resemble small boxes piled one on top of another to create a child's tower, and the sheer size of the new towers makes them out of scale with their environment. In this landscape they seem to have no regard for the past, no respect for what has gone before, and seem adolescent and over-hasty compared with the fading elderly grandeur of the district. Other new developments in the city such as Queen Square have been built invisibly into the existing landscape; they seem to respect the past and move the urban landscape into the future, not seek to overpower and dominate it.

Yet from the other end of the city, from Lime Street and William Brown Street, the new apartment blocks blend seamlessly with the existing pattern of buildings in the central business district. This is because they fit neatly into a vision of the city – of the country's cities – expounded in the 1960s and 1970s. Then, too, the old way of British city life was changing, and old industries and businesses were closing. The damage inflicted on city centres by the Blitz was not repaired 'where it was and as it was', but instead the process of demolition continued for many years after 1945. The wastelands were seen as the start of an opportunity to create modern, vibrant cities with safe 20th-century streets and improved car access. They were to be cities of tall glass towers, cities connected by fast clean motorways, cities with no murky corners or old Dickensian alleyways. In Liverpool the notorious Shankland plan would have redesigned the city on these lines, a stupendous example of what might have been. The Liverpool Inner Motorway, to give the plan its formal title, would have sent a motorway slicing deep through the heart of the city, redeveloped Georgian Rodney Street as a major thoroughfare and thrown a road on huge concrete stilts in front of the Anglican Cathedral. New buildings would have fitted in and over these new roads, which would in some cases have gone through new buildings, an echo of Fritz Lang's *Metropolis*. Some of the structures were erected, and it would make an interesting journey to connect them, the ruins of a city that was never built.

The city council orchestrated bright new homes in the sky in the 1960s, and it is ironic that at the same time that the private sector is building high-rise tower blocks, the city council has started developing streets. Much of the regeneration of the city has been done by private companies and private initiative, and it is sometimes felt that the unpopular or more outlying districts have not received the attention and financial investment they desperately need, a charge that, in fairness, is vigorously denied by the local authority. The city council have worked successfully to regenerate pockets of inner-city housing and build new schools, and, of course, have coordinated the new buildings and remodelled infrastructure. They have also redeveloped some of the worst housing in the city, a process stretching back to the slum clearances of the 1960s. Nearly half a century ago they experimented with tower blocks and rehoused council tenants in glass and metal towers on huge estates a long way away from the city they grew up in; it is a cliché of modern town planning to see this as a drastic mistake. What stopped the new model of streets-in-the-sky housing in the 1960s was the notion that communities had been destroyed by being rehoused and that new communities did not develop in the new tower blocks; instead of a better quality of life for people they were rehoused in instant slums. So today, instead of building high-rise tower blocks, the city council have retained communities by rehousing people in houses on streets, with a small garden and a driveway for the car. Whole streets of derelict housing in Toxteth and Everton have been cleared or are scheduled to be demolished, and

The Unity Building from Old Hall Street.

smart new houses have been built, creating almost micro-suburbs in the Victorian landscape. There are fewer houses per square mile, perhaps reflecting the city's lower population, and the houses are no doubt brighter, cleaner and more modern; it just seems a pity that they are built at the expense of the city's Victorian housing. However, it cannot be denied that the landmark projects and the giant apartment buildings in the city centre have been predominantly built by the private sector.

The development companies have overcome many of the problems attached to tower blocks by selling the apartments and not renting them. The residents have a vested interest in maintaining their property, and the old 'community spirit' to maintain good relations with neighbours and to maintain the property generally is replaced by a middle-class anxiety about property prices. What kept old working-class communities together and partly maintained the physical quality of the area was shared values and street living, but what maintains the modern flat is anxiety about its market value; perhaps the end result is the same. However, development companies have no interest in 'community' and no interest in the quality of urban life. The new residents of the tower blocks are seen as individuals or couples, not as members of society at large. There are no new shops in these apartment blocks, no churches or post offices, and it seems strange to even think that there should be. The question of where these people will buy a newspaper or pint of milk is almost irrelevant; they will drive to an out-of-town supermarket and drive back to park in their allotted underground parking bay, not stagger home from the city centre laden with bags of groceries. This is part of the attractive urban lifestyle that is offered or suggested to accompany the new home. In photographs designed to sell the apartments, young couples lounge on large white chairs sipping wine, gaze over the soft-focus lights of the night-time city from their glass balcony, or laugh with friends around a large dark table. There are close-ups of luscious salads and glasses of sparkling wine, but no books, no old people, no children. The rooms are modernist, austere backdrops for dinner parties or brief stopovers on the way to a night out; with their functional modern furniture and bare walls they could very well be a quiet corner of a nightclub. The new apartments seem to offer all the pleasures of city life without any of its murky inconveniences. This depiction of city life, free from the realities of the street, is an urban ideal, almost an idyll. But it is an ideal aimed at wealthy young people at a particular stage in their lives, having left their parental home but not yet having children. It has nothing to do with Liverpool; the same companies are probably selling the same ideal with the same photographs to young people in cities across Britain, and the uneasy suspicion arises that the residents never meet real Liverpudlians as they commute from IT office to apartment, or gym, or to an expensive restaurant, and never set foot on the street or meet a real person.

In any case, the city designed for the motorist is an out-of-date model for urban

*Beetham Tower reflected
on Leeds Street.*

*Quiet urban
development,
Duke Street.*

life. With climate change and pollution, the car is no longer seen as the saviour it once was, and one of the frequent complaints of city life is 'too much traffic, too many cars'. A more modern construct of city life, and perhaps the distant future for Liverpool's 'suburbs', is low-rise buildings with safe car-free streets, a mixed community of old and young, workplaces and restaurants, homes and small parks on the same street, a mosaic of family, work and social life within easy walking distance of home, a mediaeval model of urban life and a picture of Liverpool before it expanded beyond the city walls. Urban life is seen as richer for the complexities and awkwardness of street life; it is this 'edge' that gives city living its piquancy, as the American soldiers found squatting derelict New York buildings in 1945. It is the life on the street that city planners encourage but cannot buy, and it is this richness of street life which Liverpool has in abundance even today.

INDEX